DATE DUE

12/12

An Introduction to Emergency Exercise Design and Evaluation

An Introduction to Emergency Exercise Design and Evaluation

Third Edition

Robert McCreight

 Bernan Press

Lanham • Boulder • New York • London

Contents

Contents

Preface

Designing emergency exercises and developing useful mechanisms for evaluating those exercises is a mixture of art and science. The scientific aspect involves identifying the essential elements, principles, and structural issues associated with making emergency exercises worthwhile and providing practical operational value to practitioners and professionals. My aim is to help students of emergency management grasp and understand the core issues as well. The artful dimension of exercise design and evaluation is pinpointing the variables, ambiguities, and risks associated with structuring, coordinating, and evaluating complex pseudo-emergencies events meant to replicate reality. Combining the two is vital to create a valuable learning experience. With this in mind, my focus is on natural disasters and technological emergencies more so than terrorism. The book's focus is on small- to medium-size cities and those wishing to get an in-depth look at exercise design issues.

Finding a suitable guide or textbook to navigate this field of endeavor recalls the "needle in a haystack" analogy. To be sure, there are many guides and handbooks generated by state or local emergency management agencies that are helpful and instructive. However, what is needed is a textbook that includes the fundamentals and allows students and researchers to further enhance their knowledge by investigating those publications, interviewing emergency managers, observing the work of an exercise planning team, or just witnessing an actual exercise unfold. Hopefully, this book will supply the fundamentals that enable all students, practitioners and experts to agree on common terms, principles, and strategies. My emphasis is to explore both the value and purposes of scenario-based and capabilities-based exercises.

Emergency exercises address and reveal the significant gaps between plans and capabilities. More importantly, well-crafted exercises will draw attention to those areas of doctrine, staff training and operational requirements which can be validated and which deserve a second look for revision or adaptation. The overall aim of this book is to make it easier for emergency managers, emergency planners, academic leaders in emergency management, and students of emergency management to understand some of the fundamentals associated with exercise design. Seldom does one find a credible and reliable college level course which seeks to impart this information however for those who embark on that effort this book should provide a useful introduction.

The variety of exercise options available are built upon the fundamental educational principle that progressively difficult emergency exercises build effective learning, enhance comprehension, and ultimately increase emergency preparedness and operational readiness. Even with staff turnover, limited funds, and experience, some localities will seek exercises that stretch and stress their emergency responders. This book aims to help in that regard by providing specific guidance that is useful, less rigorous, and more flexible than the highly structured DHS HSEEP program.

The overall purpose of the book is to reinforce the twin notions that

1. Well-designed exercises enhance emergency readiness, verify preparedness, test emergency planning assumptions, and sharpen response functions and
2. Exercise evaluations that are comprehensive, honest, and analytical make a real difference in validating emergency preparedness and readiness if necessary changes are incorporated into EO plans and improved readiness procedures.

It is also useful to point out the merits of the "progressive" education principle embedded in the successive iteration of emergency exercise training programs. All of these approaches start with less complex emergency exercises and progress through a series of increasingly complex emergency exercises to verify preparedness and test readiness. That is how better emergency management happens—not accidentally. Of course, in any textbook odyssey, errors of omission, oversight, and commission are mine exclusively.

I want to thank all those who in recent years have been instrumental in shaping my own evolving sense of what matters and what doesn't in the growing field of emergency management. There were several key persons whose views were invaluable as I sought to revise this volume and create a second edition. I apologize for not listing them all. Some of these helpful souls include Don Donahue, Curry Mayer, Chuck Manto, Irmak Renata-Tenali, Tom Carey, and Mark Troutman. Special thanks are due for those who read early drafts of the first edition and provided invaluable comments and suggestions to improve the text—they are the experts after all—like former Maryland State Public Health Director James "Smokey" Stanton, DCFD HAZMAT Battalion Chief John Donnelly, and former Oregon State EM Director Myra Lee.

Robert McCreight

Introduction

Revisions to the first edition after its publication in 2011 have been undertaken with the aim of including new material, updates, and additional observations. In this instance I continue to advocate more complex scenarios and situations which feature high risk threats should be the focus of emergency exercises in the second and third decade of the twenty-first century. This can only be done by explicitly examining these challenges through the conduct of robust exercises. By drawing attention to unique exercise design issues at a significantly sharper level of detail my objective in supplementing the text is designed to help practitioners and students of emergency management understand obvious, subtle and indirect aspects of the exercise design process.

In the decades following 2015 there will be increased pressure on state and local governments to demonstrate that ramped up and enhanced emergency performance in response and recovery operations has benefited from prior years of experience. Well-crafted exercises can deliver on this expectation. The sheer variety of emergency challenges include natural disasters, industrial and infrastructural accidents, system failures, and terrorism. Communities should be prepared for any scenario from the simplest to the most complex and challenging.

However, not all are enthusiastic about exercises providing the "magic bullet" to enhance overall performance. Some remain doubtful that exercises alone can strengthen emergency response. Today some hesitance remains about sharing insights and lessons learned from similar tabletops, drills and sophisticated deployed exercises doubtful that such events can impart operational wisdom and applicable insights which focus on the multiplicity of operational issues involved. This regrettably remains true in the international arena as well. One goal of this book is to encourage wider sharing of exercise outcomes and insights to the benefit of all engaged in the serious pursuit of better emergency management.

   More must be done to share perspectives and isolate key operational principles where possible so that real savings in lives and property can be attained. As such, efforts will be made in this new edition to focus on relevant subjects and themes which are compelling and rightly deserve some further discussion, analysis and elaboration such as these topics which merit attention via crafted emergency exercises that primarily focus on and deal with:

• Continuity of operations
• Dealing with WMD events
• Mass casualty disasters
• Infrastructure emergencies
• Unified command
• Homeland defense
• Business continuity planning
• Complex catastrophic emergencies
• Cybersecurity emergencies
• Energy grid collapse crises
• Agrosecurity crises
• Sustained and stressed emergency operations

In the introduction to the second edition of this text published in 2016 it was strongly urged that greater attention be directed toward more complex, difficult and challenging emergency scenarios which included emphasis on mass casualty problems, homeland defense operations, cybersecurity, grid collapse, agrosecurity and catastrophic scenarios with multidimensional issues of truly strategic significance. My rationale for stressing that mix of issues was done for several reasons. First, professional emergency managers must explore the outermost edges of complexity and challenge avoiding the temptation to default to easier and more familiar problems. Second, it makes sense to consider tackling more complex emergencies and thereby enhance the response skills of emergency staff alerting leadership to the often unique issues which are triggered in challenging cutting edge scenarios. Third, it may seem obvious but stressing the emergency staff and response team with exercises which feature unexpected and tough problems of the future with an emphasis on complex catastrophes will enhance overall emergency response quality and pay real dividends in terms of better and faster response activities in more routine and simple emergencies.

   This third edition draws attention toward making future emergency exercises more challenging and complex in recognition of the variety of catastrophic scenarios we ought to prepare for in the future. The domain of "low probability—high consequence" events needs to be expanded and understood for what it legitimately contains as the old and traditional emergencies make way for the more difficult, technically complex, and multifaceted emergencies we expect to see after 2020. In making these revisions and updates it is hoped that career professionals in emergency management, current academic researchers and instructors, along with students recognize that the spectrum of risks and threats never remains static. Growing societal complexity and increased reliance on newer technology brings with it an array of novel situations and interrelationships that contain the unexpected and the unappreciated. The era of potentially catastrophic emergencies with bona fide strategic consequences and effects is upon us and we risk ignoring it at our peril. Seeing ahead a few years allows us an edge to overcome that peril that we need to exploit.

Chapter 1

Emergency Exercises

Objectives and Purpose

As a first principle, emergency exercises must validate the training of staff, enable verification of equipment and technologies, permit an objective examination of how useful an emergency plan really is, and allow a realistic demonstration of selected tasks and functions that emergency personnel and first responders are expected to display in an actual crisis. Exercises functioning at their best will test both preparedness and readiness. Preparedness refers to all the predisaster activities, training, equipping, and mitigation efforts undertaken to lessen disaster risk. *These are all the measures, procedures, training, and effort that precede actual deployment.* By contrast, readiness measures all the activities, tasks, operations, and decisions that first responders engage in *upon deployment to the crisis site*, including all essential emergency operations immediately following a disaster. Exercises must measure both to a certain extent. If an exercise does not do this, or provides a less than realistic opportunity to demonstrate critical emergency response tasks and functions, it fails to provide its primary value to managers and political leaders.

A key second principle in emergency exercises is that it must reinforce and reflect the operational requirements expected of first responders and point toward a standard of professional performance that all seek to attain. In that sense, it is crucial that emergency managers regularly test and examine their own capabilities against crisis situations ranging from the simplest to the most complex. This effort shines a light on critical support institutions, their leadership and other significant coordinating organizations which enable the community's emergency management machinery to function at its highest levels. Included in this mix are hospitals, NGOs like the Red Cross, public safety personnel, evacuation coordinators, relief transportation operators and shelter managers to name a few.

Here the core idea is to devise and continually improve upon a standard of emergency response and civil support which routinely improves upon itself and imports learning from prior experience. The definition of success is to meet normal response expectations and progressively exceed those expectations. It must be judged a failure by any measure of assessment because what was expected was not, in fact, demonstrated. Worse, exercise performance in a suboptimal setting could be mistakenly construed as satisfactory or effective when in fact it is not.

Still a third principle worth contemplating at the outset is understanding the realm and scope of emergency response operations in an age of mega-disasters and terrorism. It is important to grasp the interagency coordinating framework under which several emergency operations might be conducted. These temporary but critical ad hoc organizations meld federal, state and local emergency response experts into vertically and horizontally merged teams who coalesce around a central mission—effective emergency response, protection of life and property and setting the stage for post emergency recovery. Blended resources which may entail military, private sector and NGO elements contributing to overall response should be a focus of further study.

In the minds of emergency responders, the proof of an exercise's value is found in the degree to which it challenges their skills, stresses their team, and reinforces the array of tasks and responsibilities they are expected to demonstrate. In the minds of political leaders and average citizens, exercises must validate the expenditure of time and money required by demonstrating a response capacity and emergency management strategy that is second to none. In the final analysis, if a well-designed exercise helps responders sharpen their skills and maximize their effectiveness, then the value derived in saved lives and protected property is beyond any human measure or cherished goal. Most people in the business of emergency management clearly grasp *that exercises address and reveal the significant gaps between plans and capabilities. Moreover, if they are well designed and managed emergency exercises shine a light on critical aspects of crisis management such as, intergroup coordination, communications discipline, the importance of validation and confirmation of key tasks, leadership, decisionmaking, group problem-solving and skills related to identifying best possible options for action.*

Emergency exercises have four primary purposes: (1) to validate the assumptions and procedures of the emergency operations plan, (2) to help identify real gaps in vulnerability assessments and capability determinations (including assessments of available resources and suitable staffing), (3) to enable verification of staff preparedness and training for all-hazard emergencies, and (4) to provide realistic opportunity to verify emergency readiness. This is completely consistent with the belief that *preparedness* deals with all the preliminary training, standard operating procedures (SOPs), equipment practice, and performing of the routines of emergency response, while *readiness* is the actual demonstration of emergency response capability under deployed conditions to respond effectively to all-hazard crises. This calls for a more comprehensive assessment of staff training, key equipment, and SOPs, and the integration of systems and technologies necessary to manage an emergency situation. Simply put, an effective exercise measures whether fundamental emergency functions actually operate according to plan and whether emergency personnel know what is to be done, how to do it, and at what level of effectiveness or quality it must be done. This is the heart of the emergency management enterprise, and it brings scrutiny to the dilemma of preparedness versus readiness, enabling an accurate assessment to be made of emergency response capability. This dilemma must be clearly understood before work on emergency exercises can begin. To simply assume that preparedness equates to readiness is a misguided notion.

Preparedness is planning, development of SOPs, specification of roles and responsibilities, staging of equipment, training staff, connecting integral systems, and exhibiting masterful awareness of required actions and tasks related to an emergency response function.

Readiness is the actual demonstration and execution of essential emergency functions and tasks at the highest possible level of effectiveness in an actual crisis or in realistic emergency exercise situations.

The dilemma is that political leaders and emergency managers can never completely verify and validate preparedness and readiness for all-hazard situations and demanding crises unless they are committed to a routine, rigorous, and realistic exercise program that enables them to observe, evaluate, and improve their emergency operations. This means that a robust exercise program always includes annual strategies which stress progressive operational improvements and periodic parallel collaboration with other communities. Exercises must focus not only on the obvious and expected range of emergencies and disasters but allow teams to tackle the unexpected and deeply challenging emergency scenarios that task emergency responders in activities and decisions beyond the well-known and obvious.

A full array of appropriate exercise modes and events such as tabletops, full-field-deployed exercises, and function-specific drills (such as an emergency alert drill), along with "no-notice" exercises provide ample opportunities to test, stress, and validate the performance of emergency responders. Such activities reinforce and validate procedures, doctrine and training to an extent that qualitatively better emergency response actions can often result.

It is important to make the fundamental distinction between *scenario-based exercises* and *capabilities-based exercises* before we delve more deeply into the fundamentals. In scenario-based exercises the emphasis is primarily on the handling of an overall emergency situation bringing the entire crisis under control. An example would be either a Category 4 hurricane or a coastal earthquake measuring 7.9 where the aim is to test all the expected emergency response actions that would be required. On the other hand, capabilities-based exercises set out to examine how certain functional capabilities actually perform, such as hazmat response or the management of mass casualty incidents. The two types should be considered interchangeable as long as we recognize their primary emphasis differs in terms of focus. Too often, exercises fail to either reflect or reconstruct reality with sufficient regard for genuine demands and ongoing stress so that response capability can be determined and effective practices reinforced. It is crucial that emergency exercises be sharpened to such a challenging degree that emergency managers and first responders can actually carry out their tasks and determine firsthand whether they were being effective or not. Of course, many exercises have been successful at fostering a keener appreciation for the actual demands and exigencies of a crisis, but there is still a lingering problem with some exercises that do not challenge, do not stress, and do not levy burdensome demands on emergency workers. This also reinforces the apparent value of "no-notice" exercises to conclusively reveal how prepared and ready first responders actually are given a complex scenario they neither expected or were tacitly warned could happen in the immediate future.

Being mindful of the vast expanse of emergency situations and crises that can befall a community, it is important to consider the range of demands from day-to-day operations all the way up to a catastrophic mass-casualty disaster. Anything that can happen along that complex spectrum is literally possible, although most communities are inclined more to train and prepare for emergencies they feel are most likely to happen. The full range of possibilities can never be forgotten and must be seriously considered.

Exercise design fundamentals should focus on the full range of probable emergencies ranging from the simple to more complex situations. Consideration must be accorded the many possible emergency scenarios and situations where effective and comprehensive response by trained and dedicated emergency experts makes all the difference. Some of these examples include:

- Mass casualty exercises
- WMD effects and consequence management exercises
- Continuity of Operations (COOP) exercises
- Blended state/county/local emergency operations exercises
- Business continuity exercises

Photo 1.1   Example of earthquake damage.

Photo 1.2   Quakes, floods, and hurricane are expectable emergencies.

- Hazmat problems and exercises
- Disaster recovery and remediation exercises
- Infrastructure collapse or accident exercises
- Collaborative exercises with National Guard or military support elements

When emergency responders deploy to a chemical explosion, airplane crash, multi-vehicle collision in an ice storm, a tornado's aftermath, or the perils of rescuing people from rising flood tides, the identical array of issues arises: *Can responders do what is necessary? Can they do it effectively?* Readiness for the full variety of these typical incidents is one of the chief objectives of an emergency exercise.

It also makes sense to prepare for manageable incidents and emergencies as well as larger disasters considered extreme and catastrophic. In view of the range of options which cities and communities may face, and with due consideration of advancing technology, aged infrastructure, lingering systems vulnerabilities and turnover in political and professional leadership it is sensible to ensure that exercises be conducted on a regular and recurring basis. It is important to note that any exercise completed successfully a few years ago does not guarantee readiness for the next major emergency situation. Task repetition, novel challenges, and unique problems are the hallmarks of sophisticated emergency exercise planning.

If we are truly committed to an "all hazards" response capability that means all disasters arising from natural calamity (earthquake, hurricane, flood and wildfire) must be exercised periodically to reflect and reinforce the diversity and depth of a minimal standard of response. This further enables government to render assistance under EMAC (Emergency Management Assistance Compact) to like communities in distress. Collaborative community emergency planning enhances all entities involved and strengthens regional and county-level response. This notion can be termed a "lateral operational capability" which reinforces the principle of communities assisting each other.

This "lateral operational capability" principle applies equally to all medium sized cities and towns (whether adjacent or not) where mutual assistance expectations loom as a genuine reserve contingency. Our resident emergency managers expect this normally as a natural byproduct of contingency planning and all hazard awareness. One can never assume that an EMAC as described on paper will actually perform as stated when a genuine emergency occurs and the EMAC must be invoked. In many cases there will be minimal problems in others there may be some unpleasant surprises. Understanding how EMACs operate and what issues they bring to the surface is well worth time spent in a cordial tabletop discussion among key leaders to allow community emergency planners the opportunity to discuss them in some detail. Usually the EMAC is bilateral in nature which means each party assumes responsibility for helping the locality in need if the EMAC is invoked.

In some instances, a state legislature's formal approval is required to allow jurisdictions to cooperate in an EMAC arrangement. State law or regulation may also establish legal requirements that govern the creation and operation of aid and assistance agreements in the state generally. State-specific requirements can also affect intrastate agreements between localities and other parties, as well as interstate agreements between the state and other parties. In most cases certain specific policies, protocols, and resource definitions that govern delivery of aid have been developed. In addition to the legal requirements for administering aid, ongoing training, exercising, and updating of aid agreements and the policies and protocols implementing them is a key factor in effectively delivering mutual aid.

While every EMAC has its own particular qualities, the U.S. Department of Homeland Security has identified through NIMS a number of important elements that should generally be included in these agreements such as:

- Definitions of key terms.
- Procedures for requesting and providing aid.
- Payment, reimbursement, and allocation of costs.
- Notification procedures.
- Roles and responsibilities of individual parties.
- Protocols for interoperable communications.
- Relationships to other MAAs.

- Recognition of licensures and certifications.
- Sharing agreements.
- Workers' compensation.
- Liability and immunity.
- Provisions to update and terminate the agreement.

Formalized, pre-event aid agreements can also expedite Federal Emergency Management Agency (FEMA) reimbursement for services, equipment, and supplies delivered via mutual aid. FEMA will reimburse mutual aid costs if the aid was requested and the assistance requested directly relates to a disaster eligible for FEMA assistance, and occurred under a signed, written mutual aid agreement. The aid agreement must apply in all situations, not just triggered by a federal Stafford Act emergency/disaster declaration or that are eligible for federal aid. The entire spectrum of FEMA post disaster operations and that agency's role in recovery can be misunderstood without some deliberate discussion, including a mini-exercise, to ascertain how this stressful but necessary assistance function actually works.

The EMAC concept was ratified by the U.S. Congress in 1996 and it has been adopted by all states, the District of Columbia, and some territories. The EMAC does not replace federal assistance but acts to complement federal resources or to provide resources when an event does not warrant federal assistance. Normally, an EMAC is set in motion by a requesting state through a gubernatorial declaration of emergency and a request for assistance made through the National Emergency Management Association (NEMA), the organization that administers these EMACs. Under most EMAC documents the requesting state is responsible for compensating the assisting state for any expenses incurred while the agreement itself also addresses licensing, liability, and compensation issues for personnel deployed pursuant to an EMAC request.

Exhibiting a degree of emergency response readiness in one or few areas is satisfactory but local jurisdictions who rely on local or county emergency response assistance ordinarily expect that flexible responses geared to the variety of emergency situations makes the most sense. So, for example, in Midwestern states where tornados are routine it is essential that relevant emergency planning take place but that is far from enough. Emergency experts in Kansas can learn and repeatedly test their skills in post-tornado recovery operations but unless they are compelled to delve into other plausible scenarios that may affect them, (such as flooding and wildfires) their training and readiness will be below par. There is also considerable merit to testing the proposition that less likely scenarios that could potentially yield devastating and widespread damage are worth exploring when compared to repeated instances of rehearsals for the most likely disaster where responders, their team, and equipment are never pushed beyond the comfortable.

Exercises that continually portray the expected and familiar become danger-ously routine. This benefits nobody and leads to false confidence.

The starting point for emergency exercise design is to ask some pretty fun-damental questions, such as *how prepared and ready are we for a Category 3 hurricane?* Alternately, we can legitimately ask whether we are prepared for an F2 tornado and its aftermath. Or, *how prepared and ready are we for a mass casualty event that overwhelms our public health infrastructure?* Or bet-ter yet, *how prepared and ready are we for a radiological emergency requir-ing the hasty evacuation, shelter, and treatment of nearly 35,000 citizens and the resultant long-term contamination of schools, businesses, and homes?* In these instances, having sensible emergency plans based on realistic risk and vulnerability assessments is a good starting point. Most localities subject to catastrophic emergency or widespread disaster understand very well that their ability to respond with some effectiveness within the first seventy-two hours after the onset of the crisis is absolutely crucial. Most cities and towns already realize they are "on their own" for the first seventy-two hours, but how many know they have the capability to respond effectively in any crisis scenario possible along the all-hazard spectrum? Worse, if some localities only plan for a seventy-two-hour horizon before state and federal assistance arrives, isn't this a dangerous assumption if the crisis overwhelms their resources for upwards of five days? How do localities, even those enhanced by mutual assistance agreements, cope with a prolonged disaster when outside rein-forcement and assistance may be a week or more in coming? Does it make sense to prepare for that scenario?

For other emergencies that can be managed and cleaned up in less than eight hours, most cities and towns may feel they have adequately prepared for every contingency. Yet in even these shorter and less intense emergency scenarios the proof of preparedness and readiness is the way first respond-ers actually perform. Whether it is a short-term emergency or an extensive catastrophic event, the "no-fault" measure of preparedness and readiness is always a well-designed exercise.

Clearly, local governments have limited resources to design and perform exercises within their regional area. With mutual assistance agreements involving other jurisdictions many small towns can harness the resources of nearby communities and pool their respective suites of emergency equip-ment and personnel. FEMA has also stressed its forward looking posture in FY-2015 funding request to Congress by asking for over $7 billion in new disaster relief funding along with, further aid to Hurricane Sandy victims in multi-year recovery issues, greater emphasis on using geospatial resources, greater remedial assistance to local governments and a keen focus on being more of an "expeditionary" organization which aims to be more responsive and timely deployed to adversely affected areas. Since 2005, with significant annual funding for national level and enhanced regional exercises, FEMA estimates it has spent over $618 million on national exercises, testing scenarios that include an outbreak of pneumonic plague, chemical attacks, and dirty bombs.[1]

We also know that the Department of Homeland Security (DHS) since FY-2007 has steadily improved its own exercise program in conjunction with FEMA focused on terrorist-related incidents which target our infrastructure and attempt to exploit weaknesses in border, port, airport and other sensitive transit organizations. DHS recognizes that unique capabilities reside along our own military reserve and National Guard elements which can demonstrably assist and augment both state and local government in emerging disasters under the rubric of "homeland defense." Ongoing Defense Department efforts over since FY-2007 involving the United States Northern Command (NORTHCOM) have demonstrated the growing DoD commitment to enhancing military support, augmentation and response to ill affected state and local government to deal with complex public health crises, exceptional natural disasters like Hurricane Sandy, and unique domestic threat like those involving weapons of mass destruction.

RELATIONSHIP BETWEEN EMERGENCY PLANS AND EXERCISES

The fundamental issue to address even before an emergency exercise is contemplated is to reaffirm the connection between emergency operations plans (EOPs) and the planning required to structure and conduct an exercise. EOPs are intended to provide an overall guide outlining major facilities, buildings, risk zones, and expected hazards for which the managing, or governing, organization is responsible to safeguard. Hence, universities, cities, major commercial operations, manufacturing centers, military bases, hospitals, stadiums, and related areas where a significant concentration of people either live or work and are exposed to identified risks is the basis for an EOP.

Several basic ideas about EOPs deserve mention. First, there is the notion that EOPs can be based on several assumptions which should be rooted in real experience and best estimates of the risks a community might face. For example, from the short list described below there are several avenues worth considering.

- plans based on historical emergencies or regional emergencies
- plans based on community risk assessments going back 10 years
- plans based on expected emergency scenarios
- plans tied to community proximity to high value security/commercial sites

From this short list we see immediately the value of developing an EOP which at least considers the range of risks and threats within 100 miles of any community's downtown hub. So the starting point in EOP development is to examine whether these four areas of potential emphasis. Without a rigorous and objective assessment of this question there is a risk that the EOP will fall short of its potential.

A second idea fundamental to EOP development is the extent to which the plan itself is comprehensive enough to address multiple risk scenarios and allow for aspects of mitigation, response, recovery and resilience applicable to key risk areas. The plan can never account for all potential behaviors and contingencies so it is best to ensure the EOP addresses those most likely and allows for some explicit consideration of situations which are deemed less likely. In so doing, the EOP reflects careful consideration of the true array of emergency situations which could confront the community. This aspect of the plan explains which resources and capabilities are inherently local and where outside augmentation from neighboring communities, the state, the military and the private sector may be needed.

Finally, a third key aspect of EOP development is to always consider the full range of public and private entities and infrastructure at risk with due regard for spelling out the expected actions, capabilities and possible shortfalls which may arise contingent on the type of emergency situation being confronted. Here, gathering inputs and advisory assistance from key public and private organizations in your community ensures that most crucial considerations and variables have been incorporated into the EOP.

An additional consideration in EOP development which deserves deeper reflection is the degree to which an EOP should outline and identify the risk scenarios most likely to affect the community and inflict the most significantly adverse effects on its citizens and businesses. Here, the task is simply to label those emergency situations, especially natural disasters, where the history and experience of emergency risk seems greatest for the community involved, such as

- flash floods
- tornados
- earthquakes
- wildfires
- hurricanes

Design considerations in drafting an EOP would rest on direct consideration of these basic emergency scenarios and they should be relatively ranked from lowest to highest probability with due regard for the available emergency resources and latent response capacity which a community can commit

Relationship Between Emergency Plans and Exercise Design

Emergency Plans [EOP]

Identify the scope, purpose, assumptions, capabilities, vulnerabilities, at-risk infrastructures, emergency tasks, response operations, EOC duties and special situational annexes related to a government, business, college campus, or other public facility

Exercise Design & Evaluation

Tests the operational requirements, key tasks, assumptions, equipment, technologies, procedures, and response operations outlined In emergency plans

Figure 1.1   Relatioship Between Emergency Plans and Exercise Design.

to a disaster event. Knowing that an EOP cannot cover every conceivable emergency situation it makes sense to guarantee that the most likely events are duly recognized and form the basis for a relevant EOP.

The first objective of an EOP is to identify the risk and hazard issues for the territorial space that the organization, group, business, or government retains responsibility to protect and safeguard. It should also provide guidance to inhabitants, employees, visitors, and all who enter the risk domain and territory covered by the EOP on what to do and how to behave in different risk, hazard, or crisis situations. It makes sense that these plans be integrated with and coordinated with major commercial and business enterprises, major social organizations, and civic groups to ensure they are complementary and provide evidence of congruent concept and purpose.

Good EOPs will outline the protective steps necessary for reacting to an emergency event and they will usually identify which organizational unit is primarily responsible for responding to the crisis and getting it under control. EOP guidance will be written for *two different audiences*—innocent unsuspecting victims of the crisis versus the trained, skilled, and specially equipped emergency rescue workers and responders.

When compared to the elements of an Exercise Plan (ExPlan), it is apparent that the objectives of the two plans are very different. The *ExPlan* is an outline of how the emergency rescue workers and first responders decide to handle the crisis. It may involve a well-known situation like orderly evacuation of a dormitory or office building given a bomb threat, or it may be very complex with unique and unexpected aspects such as how to protect workers in the upper floors of a thirty-story building when toxic fumes are enveloping the air-handling system or how to protect and evacuate a town when a major railway tanker spill spreads a cloud of chlorine gas into the town's commercial district.

What matters most is that we understand the distinction between an EOP and the ExPlan along with grasping how different their fundamental purposes are. The EOP provides the predisaster guidance outlining what safety measures and protective actions can be completed given an emergency situation. The ExPlan outlines how a group of emergency workers and first responders will be expected to handle and overcome an emergency situation which is carefully described as a testable challenge to validate and confirm how emergency response will actually perform consistent with EOP and professional standards. Figure 1.1 underscores the crucial fact that roles and responsibilities are delineated by EOPs while exercises are designed to test them.

OBJECTIVES AND PURPOSE

Exercises must have objectives and serve an operational purpose. If the focus of the exercise is to determine how prepared first responders are to handle an airplane crash, a Category 3 hurricane, a chemical explosion, or a complex hazmat event at a major downtown intersection, the overall aims remain identical. The objective simply is to assess how quickly, how effectively, and how comprehensively the *first responders as a team, together with their supporting and coordinating agencies and resources*, perform their assigned tasks and execute their primary emergency functions. In that case, all the requisite tasks and collaborative actions that individuals and groups engage in will be under scrutiny. Both the tasks expected and those tasks related to problem solving and the unexpected are to be examined with equal concern. Often multiple agencies may be involved in the response where coordination among them is the key issue. Some mutual assistance agreements will bring firefighting units from different towns together and the collaboration they exhibit in handling the crisis is the key.

Often in such arrangements or in ordinary deployments to tackle an emergency, first responders will find themselves adjacent to the "edge" of another's territory, mission, or functional space. Police and firefighters may overlap in their responsibilities to clear a shopping mall of innocent shoppers where a blaze has broken out, or they may find themselves engaged in similar duties involving a disaster at a large sports complex where hasty evacuations are required. This happens very often and is part of emergency response processes. In fact, the sheer numbers of responders when blended with the size and scale of the disaster makes the situation inherently more difficult and dangerous. Management of the event by senior officials coordinating their instructions and synchronizing their operations, issuing on-scene instructions, tackling problems, and resolving roadblocks are all fair game. So it makes sense when designing an exercise that as many of these issues as possible should be replicated in the exercise test event.

The objectives for any exercise must be challenging yet achievable and should reflect the array of fundamental tasks and activities expected of first responders in a given emergency scenario or crisis event. Objectives should primarily be structured and arranged to test and validate the assumptions and instructions contained in the jurisdiction's (organization's) emergency plan. Exercises can verify whether the details, the SOP, and relevant technical guidance are sufficient, obsolete, irrelevant, or superfluous. Of course, exercise can have multiple objectives, which entail primary emergency response functions like cordoning off hazard and safe zones, searching for possible missing victims, suppressing fire or explosive dangers in secured areas, and similar tasks. These functional areas of focus help determine which emergency element actually performs the task and enables them to demonstrate whether this is a solitary or shared responsibility. An exercise that allows first responders to demonstrate their knowledge and mastery of essential tasks is useful and inherently necessary. However, an exercise that pushes emergency personnel into more challenging, ambiguous, and difficult areas that raise novel issues is even more useful. This is especially true if the extra burdens in the exercise are realistic and first responders see themselves as responsible for meeting the new challenge. For example, emergency responders may feel very comfortable exercising an explosion with casualties at a local high school where the scenario is manageable and the outcomes fairly certain. However, they would be much more challenged dealing with an expedient hospital evacuation scenario where the staff and patients must be relocated because of their proximity to an uncertain, highly dangerous, and sustained hazmat crisis on a nearby major interstate highway and where other related risks are made more ambiguous by the sheer number and variety of divergent emergency resources assembled for the crisis.

Another area of controversy is the extent to which ordinary citizens and elements of the private sector are intimately involved in exercises either as players, responders, or "victims" for first responders to rescue and relocate. Decisions should be made carefully about whether the exercise promotes community involvement and private sector "buy-in" by including these groups or whether they somehow inhibit the goals of the exercise. Certainly a strong case can be made for their involvement because they (1) appreciate the

Deriving Exercise Objectives

1. Examine an agency's current emergency plans and special annexes
2. Look for previous gaps, weaknesses, or areas of concern
3. What have previous exercises revealed?
4. Can we test levels of staff knowledge of SOPs and training? Can existing staff effectively manage the basic tasks and duties required?
5. Can we test knowledge of functions, roles, and key tasks?
6. Can we test equipment/technology interface and performance?
7. Can we examine responder ability to resolve unexpected problems?
8. Can we display and sustain effective performance for seventy-two hours?
9. How prepared are we for most likely versus least likely disaster scenarios?
10. Do we really know the stress and pressure limits on our responder team?

work of first responders because of the experience, (2) understand their own unique role in a crisis, (3) grasp what the implications are for the community if emergency capabilities are not periodically strengthened, and (4) gain insights about the complexities of emergency response operations.

While a significant degree of specificity and structure is provided by DHS in its detailed Homeland Security Exercise and Evaluation Program (HSEEP) system guidance, the processes and steps discussed in this book are intended to help both students and practitioners understand the building blocks of exercise design so that exercises of all types can be constructed and used by communities with limited resources and equipment. HSEEP has its own system and is much more rigorously defined than here.

Designing actual exercise objectives can be done by the emergency manager, a team of experts chosen by the manager, outside consultants hired to advise the manager, or any mix of talent drawn from that array. Keeping evaluators and response cell staff separate is key.

Often, we have learned that comparatively better exercises can emerge from a team approach where a mixture of experienced and less experienced staff merge their perspectives into the development of a credible scenario with delineated objectives to measure the actual preparedness and readiness of the response resources to be tested. For example, if we already know the emergency operations center (EOC) functions very well, then there is no reason to test it again and again unless staff turnover and misplaced confidence indicates a new exercise would somehow reveal unexpected flaws. Nevertheless, periodic testing of the EOC makes sense. By the same token exercises that repeatedly test how the fire department will respond to an isolated tanker spill with toxic plume risks *can never satisfactorily address* whether the

What Do Exercise Objectives Look Like?

Draft Objective: (Overall Objective)

Test activation of the county operations warning system

Potential Specific Objectives:

- Test activation of the warning system through issuance of test messages using conventional dissemination methods and media.
- Test information outlets to confirm citizen receipt/understanding within two hours of issuance.
- Track and monitor message delivery within emergency response community.
- Provide staff with an opportunity to practice issuing notices and verifying their receipt.
- Send test activation messages to target groups to verify receipt and understanding.
- Test and maintain effective two-way communications to emergency staff in warning period.
- Verify on-scene command connectivity between EOC and deployed incident command system (ICS) team.

fire department can tackle a more complex multi-railcar accident and spill, involving diverse support and interdependent reliance on multiple agencies and resources, where the toxic gas escaping offers new and unexpected technical, ambiguous, and ambient hazard issues.

With each key objective outlined there must be a corresponding measurement method that enables verification and tracking of the assigned task and a parallel method to verify task completion at a delineated level of quality. It is important to structure exercises so that individual tasks and related functional responsibilities can be observed and their genuine performance evaluated. If trainees, first responders and emergency managers are never asked to actually implement their SOPs, test their equipment, or demonstrate how they would assemble as a team to perform critical emergency functions, it will never be discerned until an actual emergency occurs whether or not they are prepared and ready.

A well-designed and thoughtful exercise will answer these questions and reveal where emergency performance is impressive, marginal, or weak. It does so without loss of life and without further calamity because steps were taken as part of the exercise design process to ensure that the exercise event is realistic and exerts genuine demands on emergency personnel to display and demonstrate performance of critical tasks and functions. Effective exercises are not ambiguous about the emergency tasks to be tested or the functions to be demonstrated but focus specifically on how well, how rapidly, and how professionally emergency tasks are performed and completed.

To further illustrate the value of planning ahead, consider the constraints on a typical town's emergency manager. Often that person lacks time and resources to create an exercise team and risks a "do-it-yourself" approach, thereby thwarting the goal of objectivity that is crucial to the exercise-building process. Objectivity is needed because certain emergency functions may be favored simply to highlight the performance of better emergency response elements like fire services or EMTs rather than shed light on areas where marginal performance, ambiguity, and uncertainty might reveal some functions as lacking in quality or effectiveness.

Specificity is needed because handling complex hazmat emergencies will often call for new and unique kinds of emergency response actions that a post-tornado response would never reveal. The goal is to stress the emergency response teams in ways that enhance their ability to perform routine critical tasks at the highest level of quality while challenging them to act creatively and exhibit innovation in responding to novel or unexpected situations. Balancing the day-to-day demands and needs of many small community emergency staffs with the resource demands of an exercise will not be easy, but efforts should be made—even to include pooling resources within a specified area of mutual assistance agreements—to provide the training and insights that only exercises can offer. Remember also to balance the expected with the unexpected so that players are stressed to deal with new and difficult situations. Good exercise design will incorporate this in any exercise because proving you can perform routine functions well is only half the battle.

Finally, in creating a team of exercise designers it is more important to find experience than numbers of contributors in building an exercise. Teams can be small and seldom have to be more than five people. They can often work well with only two as long as the persons involved are willing to accept the basic principle that *stressing routine emergency response functions is only half of the problem*—presenting novel, challenging, and unusual situations that make responders think and exhibit effective innovation is just as important. *You want to see people do the right thing, the right way, and devise a creative and effective solution if there is no right way.* Likewise, in designing the exercise, identifying what key tasks and functions must be evaluated and observed along with outlining what criterion of quality best fits each task and function are among the most essential elements to include. Typically, this can be best illustrated by an exercise that explicitly seeks to demonstrate readiness for emergency responders in both their strongest and weakest areas of performance. Here the target behaviors to elicit are responders intuitively knowing when they have done a quality job on their best and strongest emergency functions and transfer of learning, patterning of key tasks, and related actions eventually carrying over into the areas where responders are weakest. *We also understand that very often mistakes and errors in an exercise become highly valuable if they illuminate a weakness or reveal an unsupportable notion that has to be studied closely to be understood.* In some cases, exercise failures are better than successes because they identify an issue that needs fixing before an actual emergency occurs.

It is also worth considering that exercise designers often make very good evaluators because they have included criteria for effective performance in the schedule of tasks, injected events, and simulated situations that form the heart of the exercise itself. Although it is important that evaluators and designers bring at least ten years of experience to the exercise design process, it may be difficult for some communities to find that degree of talent and experience. However, anything less may weaken the exercise itself.

Again, it is crucial to stress that nothing contained in this book departs from the fundamentals that the National Response Framework (NRF) and the National Incident Management System (NIMS) expect but focuses instead on fundamentals of exercise design consistent with those standards that most cities and states must comply with in order to get federal assistance. Likewise, conformance with HSEEP is recommended if the local community wants to avail itself of the structured federal exercise design system intended to assist emergency planners and bring them into alignment with FEMA and DHS requirements. Having said that, many key infrastructures such as energy companies, transportation firms, telecommunications corporations, and hospitals have decided to develop guidance on exercise planning for their staff to introduce and supplement what DHS and FEMA have already done.[2]

There's little doubt that smaller jurisdictions with limited staff may impose a significant burden on emergency managers who must become in effect a design team of one; however, in the Internet age, many draft plans can be shared with others for reviews and comment to extract beneficial perspectives and insights necessary to fashion an effective emergency management plan. There may also be opportunities to test the contributing role of nongovernmental organizations and service agencies to determine how well they are prepared for certain emergencies.

Principles for Exercise Design Team and Leaders

should have significant exercise design experience
should review proven exercise plans for other locales
should deliberately stress weakest and strongest elements
should develop the key factors and criteria for evaluation
should assist or lead exercise evaluators
should be trusted to contribute to a professional and accurate AAR

It is important to emphasize that the guidance in this book can be used by institutions, organizations and infrastructures other than conventional emergency management agencies. Adapting the material for use by these diverse groups makes sense when encountering the issue of engaging your own staff and managerial personnel in the questions: *What kinds of emergencies could happen here? What should we be prepared to do when they occur?* Here are some examples of organizations that could benefit from the instructions and guidance in this book:

- hospitals and public health facilities
- high schools and day care centers
- universities and colleges
- energy companies
- telecommunications companies
- petrochemical industries
- church groups and community organizations
- commercial manufacturing facilities
- retail communities and shopping malls

A final introductory note for this chapter must deal with the question of how a well-designed exercise actually helps verify that an acceptable level of professional behavior and operational response can be witnessed and observed. In turn, this assumes that a well-known and generally accepted standard for emergency response actions and behavior exists. Often standards for handling substantially difficult emergencies may not exist or there may lack consensus on how best to confront them. We must reckon with the harsh reality that no every solution to a complex emergency is sealed away in an experts toolbox. There will be horrendously complex emergencies that lack any tested response strategy. However, many will mistakenly believe that all possible contingent solutions and emergency responses have been devised. This is often not the case in some ambiguous or exceedingly challenging scenarios such as, just to name a few.

- mass casualty events with more than 500 victims each in multiple cities
- pandemics with novel diseases that cannot be curtailed or controlled
- extensive biological and radiological accidents or terror attacks
- massive cyber disruptions and space-based collapse of our electric grid
- superstorms devastating adjoining states destroying infrastructure

In such cases, there is the often expressed expectation that some form of federal augmentation and special assistance will be available to contain or control the offending disaster. However, it must be underscored that despite assurances that most communities should prepare for managing their own disasters for a period up to 72 hours after the initial emergency there remains concern that in some catastrophic situations outside augmentation and help may be weeks away. Planning inside the EOP, and for those who must devise coherent ExPlans, has to somehow allow room for the potential unfolding of an unforeseen disaster of catastrophic proportions.

This has been a general introduction to exercise design and evaluation. Many more specific and in-depth aspects will be covered in subsequent chapters. The central issue is one of developing confidence in determining what type of exercise, what kinds of scenarios, what sorts of task challenges, which performance criteria, and what emergency response outcomes appear to best fit the situation in your community or city. Other chapters to follow will outline the key design steps and provide useful examples that will enable better understanding of the emergency exercise design process and reveal pathways toward constructing useful exercises aimed at improving emergency response.

DISCUSSION QUESTIONS

1. What are the two primary purposes of an exercise? Are there any others?
2. What is the best starting point for emergency exercise design? Why?
3. What matters most in structuring exercise objectives?
4. What is the value and importance of a "no-notice" exercise?
5. Who should be involved in exercise development? Why?
6. What four assumptions should undergird EOP development?

RESEARCH—YOU TRY IT—RESEARCH TASKS

1. Write three separate exercise objectives related to hazmat readiness.
2. Download and read a local government's EOP—identify key issues.
3. How would you structure an exercise design team? Who would be involved?

NOTES

1. Spencer S. Hsu, "National disaster exercises, called too costly and scripted, may be scaled back," *Washington Post*, April 2, 2010: A01.
2. Tracy Knippenburg Gillis, *Emergency Exercise Handbook: Evaluate and Integrate Your Company's Plan* (Tulsa, OK: Penwell Books, 1995); Public Health Emergency Tool-kit, available at: www.nursing.columbia.edu/pdf/PublicHealthBooklet_060803.pdf.

Chapter 2

Essential Exercise Design Elements and Steps

Emergency exercise design involves several key steps and includes essential design elements. In almost every situation, anyone who attempts to formulate an effective exercise design of whatever type will likely find his or her efforts somewhat lacking unless careful consideration is given to certain basic questions. These questions include:

1. What specific emergency function needs to be tested? What roles and responsibilities?
2. What type of exercise will best enable a test of this function?
3. What are the essential conditions, requirements, procedures, and standards involved?
4. Will specific or unique equipment be needed?
5. Will specific training be needed beforehand? If so, what kind?
6. Will the assigned exercise require enactment of proven, routine, and required tasks?
7. Will the assigned exercise require problem solving and significant ad hoc action?
8. Is there a part of the emergency plan that has never been tested?
9. Are there new, unexpected or novel emergency issues that should be exercised?
10. Has the EOC ever been tested? Incident Command? Multijurisdictional deployments?

These questions are the fundamental array of considerations a serious emergency exercise designer ought to raise as preliminary plans for an exercise design are formulated. References to the nationally known Emergency

Support Functions (ESF) array of activities can also help people identify what specific functional areas of responsibility have been enumerated. Likewise, the DHS Target Capabilities List (TCL), NIMS (National Incident Management System) functional requirements and NIPP (National Infrastructure Protection Plans) outlines in significant detail the exact capabilities expected by each functional area in emergency response activities.[1]

In some cases the focus of the exercise is on team performance in a deployed emergency setting, in other instances the focus is on collaborative communication, identifying further operational support needs or verification of key data enabling on the spot decisions. A well-designed exercise hones in on these areas of specific activity and examines how tasks are carried out against a well known standard of professional emergency response. As one might expect, the greater the scale of complexity and ambiguous demands the greater the burden on exercise designers to identify and extract the kinds of observational data which affirms emergency response readiness as well as gaps and areas for onward remedial action.

Surely one can see the difference between an emergency exercise that tests a firefighter's ability to contain and control a unitary vehicle fire at a fixed site versus a paper goods warehouse fire adjacent to a major highway versus a complex hazmat spill and train wreck multi-car fire where multiple agencies, resources, and levels of government could be involved. Each situation is progressively more difficult and each requires the firefighter to engage the crisis with greater intensity of effort, perhaps more technology, and certainly more energy and imagination than the simplest crisis. While each emergency situation involves firefighting, fire suppression, and its eventual elimination, the level of complexity, magnitude of the problem, scope of emergency response, and the degree of additional skills and special tasks needed varies inversely with the size and scale of the emergency itself. It would be fair to argue that some first responders who successfully put out a vehicle fire could be completely unprepared for, or even overwhelmed by, a petrochemical plant explosion and release of different toxic fumes absent sufficient specialized training and experience. But we would not be sure unless we tested the hypothesis. *Only an effectively engineered exercise that replicates the actual crisis situation permits judgments to be made about whether first responders know what to do and how to do it effectively.* It is here that a well-designed exercise enables us to answer the question and creates a safe environment for emergency response skills to be demonstrated. Without such a test and an opportunity for firefighters to apply their special training or demonstrate their skills in using special firefighting equipment, one would never know if they were in fact prepared and ready for this crisis situation. Only a real crisis with genuine life-and-death issues would prove the question—but why do this when an exercise reveals the answers being sought?

EXAMINING THE PROCESS OF EXERCISE DESIGN

We have established that exercise design aims to fulfill certain preparedness and readiness goals. We also know that exercises can examine how tasks, clusters of tasks, functions, equipment operation, problem solving, communications, application of standardized response technologies, and other significant response team behaviors can be tested through the exercise process in a "no-notice" way to sharpen preparedness and ramp up readiness. Asking the fundamental questions outlined at the beginning of this chapter is an excellent starting point.

Any number of unique challenges can also be identified as one embarks on serious exercise design assumptions. These important issues require some further thought as they will have a profound impact on the ultimate structure of design considerations. Some of these matters deserving serious consideration as part of exercise design are

- does the exercise measure and test equipment reliability?
- does the exercise focus on key aspects of team performance?
- does the exercise test and stress crisis communications?
- does the exercise test and measure coordination with state agencies?
- does the exercise test and measure coordination with federal agencies?

Of course, many emergency managers will also have access to a rich history of prior exercises and after-action reports (AARs) to review and utilize as a basis for further preparedness and readiness testing. Many can also turn to the Lessons Learned Information System (LLIS) for some background information drawn from the emergency experiences of other towns and cities.[2]

If your city or jurisdiction does not have this operational test history, maybe other counties will, or the state emergency management agency will, or the state university that teaches bachelor's and master's degree candidates about emergency management. Ultimately, assistance from FEMA or the military's NORTHCOM headquarters in Colorado Springs may be tapped to further strengthen the array of tasks and functions you wish to see tested in an exercise. There may even be some exercises that cities would want to run in conjunction with a nearby military installation or a petrochemical plant to further enhance awareness of respective capabilities and threat dynamics affecting emergency response performance.

Many emergency managers would want to test the efficacy of the emergency plan (EOP) itself and run several challenging scenarios against the assumptions, procedures, and guidance outlined in the plan to verify whether the initial planning perspectives seem valid. This is fairly fundamental but deserves careful thought, as some people may find it both surprising and shocking that emergency plans are often not exercised at all but instead are taken for granted as documented proof that a city or town appears ready for anything simply because the plan covers the emergency situation in the text of the plan itself.

Related to this issue is the question of updating, revising and refocusing the scope of EOP activities reflective of new risk or threat issues and operational requirements which have arisen since the original EOP was developed. This may entail, for example, coverage of new industrial facilities, new hazmat risk issues, or other changes in the immediate environment of the community which merit EOP revisions. Two areas of recent focus and relatively new attention deal with cooperative plans to work with major industries in the community which might need to test and validate their own Business Continuity Plans (BCP) or in communities proximate to a major college or university there may exist a need to coordinate emergency planning as it may affect both the campus and the adjoining community.

Overall, there are a few good places to formulate a starting point for developing and constructing an exercise. Some of these initial issues should be examined by the emergency manager and his support team of experts before the outlines of an exercise design are put together. These are meant to be helpful suggestions of proven value and they include the following initial considerations.

The next critical step involves determining whether you want to test and validate certain tasks, certain complex functions, particular operations, control and operation of key technologies and equipment, ad hoc problem solving or the orchestration and integration of complex multi-agency operations. In this case, you are trying to determine what realistic test situation best

Some Initial Steps in the Exercise Planning Process

- Examine the community's current stage of emergency preparedness.
- Identify significant gaps, weaknesses, or areas of concern.
- Highlight tasks and functions where prior performance was marginal.
- Determine level and depth of first responder and EOC training and experience.
- Determine how well all staff understand their emergency preparedness roles.
- Identify what specific areas of emergency response seem weakest.
- Target emergency response functions and responsibilities appearing to be subpar.
- Examine how confident first responders are in tackling an unexpected emergency.

exemplifies how first responders and emergency staff will actually behave during an emergency. The key challenge is to replicate that emergency situation to such a degree of realism that outside experts and observers can confirm whether the response behavior was at a desirable level of quality and effectiveness while the emergency workers themselves experience a level of realistic training and undergo realistic challenges that sharpen their preparedness for a genuine emergency.

Let's take a closer look at the actual exercise design process and break down its component parts to confirm our understanding of what needs to take place and the significance of the order of events that allows the exercise designer to have confidence that they have produced a worthwhile product. What matters most in the initial phase of exercise design is an appreciation for realism and the fact that emergency responders really want to have their training validated by undergoing a rigorous and authentic test of their overall preparedness. Placing these skilled responders in a situation that actually demonstrates they are ready to perform the emergency tasks expected of them pushes them to a level of *progressive professionalism* where their confidence in performing the emergency mission assigned becomes a reinforcing element critical to their basic skills and training. The sense of pride and accomplishment derived from a well-run exercise allows emergency responders to publicly and openly affirm their special expertise in a way that also strengthens team performance and *esprit de corps*. The steps summarized in the chart below outline the most important aspects of exercise design and should be followed carefully.

Here the *first step* entails review of the emergency plan itself, and this would include a review of prior exercises; an in-depth look at prior exercise evaluations and AARs; review of LLIS documents; and the solicitation of outside expert views to identify the actual strengths, weaknesses, performance issues, and problems that have arisen in prior exercises. Without this, starting from scratch with no prior history or insight, the emergency manager has to determine which critical emergency functions need to be tested to establish a fair baseline of emergency response performance.

The *second step* involves identification of *specific capability needs or shortfalls based upon known or suspected gaps in mission performance* that need to be strengthened or improved as well as selection of a competent design team to help identify which tasks, functions, behaviors, and other activities must be included in the exercise to demonstrate that identified problems, shortfalls, or weaknesses are properly addressed. This design team will take responsibility for ensuring that key tasks and functions, or equipment operations and problem solving events, are part of the foundation of the exercise, and they will be instrumental in specifying what realistic training and situational challenges ought to be in the exercise itself. An important aspect

Figure 2.1   Exercise Design Steps.

of this step is to examine new threats and risks to the community, as well as historical emergency data, to ascertain whether the needs and issues to be exercised ought to incorporate these elements.

The *third step* is to examine and *evaluate the expected capability of the emergency staff and first responders in handling the task, function, or situational challenge that forms the basis of the exercise.* This is the most critical step for three reasons: (1) to verify levels of responder training, (2) to establish a baseline of actual performance, and (3) to confirm that this task is currently being performed at a level of quality and effectiveness that is *less than optimal.* This is crucial because the exercise aims to sharpen the behavior and performance of first responders in specific areas where the level of emergency response is not yet demonstrated at the highest level of quality. There is an opportunity to compare performance levels and expectations with those of similar cities or with a similar emergency cadre to derive some basis for the criteria to be used, but in all cases a tilt toward objective professional standards must be the norm. There is little need to test first responders and emergency workers on areas of performance where they have amply demonstrated high levels of effectiveness—instead the focus is on bringing up the overall quality of response in areas where responders are weakest and need additional training or in situations that are unfamiliar and unexpected, where responders can demonstrate their problem-solving skills. Testing responders against new or novel situations is important. One additional determinant of this step is to prudently assess whether the functions and operational tasks to be exercised will likely involve collaboration with state or federal agencies, whether it will entail some coordination with expected military support and whether industrial and business continuity issues may be involved.

The *fourth step* is to have the exercise design team settle on the type of exercise that best fits the situation and decide whether the exercise structure chosen allows first responders to actually demonstrate their skills and handling the emergency. This can be a demonstration of newly acquired skills, or skills left untested since the last exercise, or skills that have been largely dormant for a long period. Here the choices typically range from a tabletop discussion exercise to a drill, or ultimately a functional deployed exercise. Of course, there are other exercise design options, but these are most prevalent because they lend themselves to easy observation, control, and evaluation. A tabletop puts managers, team leaders, and key emergency responders around a table that simulates the crisis, and as they move through different timed phases of the event, each person describes what should be done, how it should be done, and who should be doing it. The drill asks first responders to physically demonstrate on-site their ability to perform key tasks and functions under the watchful eye of observers and evaluators, where behaviors are videotaped and key functions acted out and emergency responders are expected to complete their tasks illustrating their command of the situation and resolution of the crisis. The deployed functional exercise goes beyond this situation because it is typically a surprise and very elaborate "no-notice" event where first responders actually deploy to a simulated crisis situation, engage in sustained operations and communications activities, and are ordinarily stressed to resolve the crisis satisfactorily. In this setting responders get further complex tasks and additional injected problems to handle in the midst of the primary crisis.

In each case the type of exercise chosen reflects a level of planning, realism, progressive complexity, and sophistication needed to demonstrate first responder preparedness and readiness. It is also important that player skills should be tested under stressful conditions and demanding circumstances. It makes sense that a community's cadre of emergency responders should be challenged far beyond the rudimentary activities expected in a tabletop exercise and that preparations to conduct drills and full-scale deployed functional exercises should happen at least annually.

The *fifth step* involves exercise structure and schedule considerations. Here the key issue is to decide whether the exercise will involve a half day, a full day, or several days and whether the exercise "days" will correspond in real time to real days or fractions of days or accelerated days. Will the exercise simulate reality by running 24/7 to further stress the responders, or will it be phased over a "three-day" period condensed into a very busy one-day nine-hour exercise where every three hours reflects passage of a day? These design issues should be settled here so that subsequent steps will make sense and flow more evenly into the overall design. This is also the step where *basic exercise objectives* are determined. Here the main thrust of effort is to identify what specific tasks, functions, operations, or activities the exercise is intended to test:

- first responders dealing with flood threats
- first responders assisting in evacuation of special needs persons
- first responders dealing with a mass casualty event
- first responders assisting elementary schools in an active-shooter situation

If it is not clear to first responders what must be done—how to do it effectively—and how to do it with the least secondary risk or harm to innocent civilians, then this must be exercised. Is the exercise aimed at discovering how a firefighter unit handles a chemical explosion? Will the exercise test an elected official's skills in handling crisis communications? Is the exercise aimed at discerning how a town will respond to threats of an impending tornado? Will the exercise test the role of police, firefighters, and others in handling a major hazmat event adjacent to the city's high school or community college? Will the exercise test firefighter and emergency response to a plane crash hitting a manufacturing plant? These basic questions must be addressed during this step.

In this step, often consideration will be given to the *National Firefighter Protection Association (NFPA)* standards for determining if a particular emergency response operation meets these requirements.[3] However, one learns from exercises for example whether only four minutes of decontamination wash for people is sufficient in a highly congested environment when the NFPA may recommend washes three times longer in a radiological release emergency. In addition, many community EOPs may either be *explicit or silent about shelter-in-place and evacuation* without knowing how elaborate and difficult this is to implement. People may not grasp the significance of either alternative, depending upon their exact status when the emergency happens. Only a rigorous exercise involving civilians and first responders will provide a glimpse into all so they understand what to do and why—or not.

Some complex and extensive exercises may have several objectives that must be tested and examined. The design team and exercise players must agree beforehand on the exercise objectives and what the likely expectations are for their performance.

The *sixth step* is writing the *Master Scenario Events List (MSEL)*, which summarizes the overall exercise objectives; outlines the emergency tasks and functions to be tested; and specifies the messages and injects and taskers (i.e., additional complications) to be assigned and their timed introduction into the exercise. The purpose of a MSEL is to describe the timing and scheduling of critical exercise events, identifies the exercise controllers and evaluators, specifies how messages will be transmitted and handled, and indicates whether the exercise will be scripted or "free-play." MSELs will have enumerated columns to denote the tasker, incident inject time, function to which the tasker is assigned, expected outcomes, and any other relevant guidance for evaluators to use. In addition, MSELs often provide the overall metrics for determining what high-quality behaviors and effective performance indicators of key emergency functions might look like. Typically, MSELs are retained exclusively by exercise controllers to provide the overall schedule and strategy for the exercise. MSELs are not shared with anyone prior to or during the exercise itself. Ordinarily, evaluators and exercise controllers will be privy to the MSEL and all scheduled taskers and injects so that a proper evaluation of expected outcomes can be rendered. Sometimes it is not until well after the exercise is concluded that evaluators can assess how first responders behaved but also whether exercise controllers were inherently fair and reasonable in their exercise management activities.

Ordinarily, MSELs contain an elaborately detailed scenario that depicts the situation triggering the exercise and outlines the specific and ambiguous

Exercise Design Objectives

Design simulated activities to assess ...

-- functional responsibilities and key relationships

-- target task completion

-- logistical-technological resource dynamics

-- communication patterns

-- problem solving

-- overall readiness and preparedness

-- whether significant vulnerabilities have been ameliorated

--successful emergency response performance [realistic metrics]

Demonstrate capabilities to effectively respond to a variety of crisis scenarios and successfully manage an end to the crisis

Figure 2.2   **Exercise Design Objectives.**

aspects of the emergency to be addressed. It is important to blend realism and authenticity with some reasonable ambiguity in drafting scenarios so that exercise players understand that not every aspect of any incident is either predictable or full of clearly understood environmental facts. Weather, location, time of day, and differences among the victimized population are typically ambiguous, although we know they can have a tremendous impact in real life. Real facts should remain as real facts so that emergency responders can sort out the genuine from the fuzzy in determining what approaches make sense. Always encourage players in exercises *not to fight the scenario*—it can undermine the best of exercises and leave those involved feeling disrespected or insulted.

Looking at a typical MSEL page, one understanding that immediately arises is that the MSEL provides the organizing structure and schedule of key events, taskers, problems, and activities that players must resolve and complete using a combination of their training, intelligence, and team resources and the integrated application of best emergency practices knowledge. MSELs cannot provide the "right answer" they can only provide a suggestion of what a sensible and appropriate emergency response should be. The first responders actually performing during the exercise will demonstrate either that they can or that they cannot fulfill the special emergency requirement and satisfy the performance metrics expected of them. MSELs only outline the expected minimum response; they often cannot provide the complete and comprehensive performance metrics expected unless a widely acceptable professional standard is available to test matters such as response time to an incident following emergency alert.

The *seventh step* is the design and overall structure of the scenario itself, which includes specific *taskers and injects*. Taskers and injects are either new situations, new problems, new requirements, or new facts designed to further complicate the actions of first responders and challenge them in the

[Review—MSEL Master Scenario Events List]

- MSEL describes a situation or problem
- MSEL is intended to elicit 'correct response'
- MSEL is designed to test preparedness and readiness
- MSEL expected to validate performance
- MSEL can text both individuals and teams
- MSEL depicts all events from STARTEX to ENDEX

> At 9:45 a call identifies 3 simultaneous explosions within and adjacent to the city's major petrochemical plant. The plant's safety officer reports 10 minutes later that further explosions might occur and it cannot yet be determined if the explosions are accidental or deliberate attacks. Huge holding tanks containing 13,000 gallons of chlorine, sulfuric acid, and benzene are within 30 yards of initial explosions. Residences housing approximately 9,000 people are within one mile of the facility gate. What needs to be done?

Figure 2.3   Review—MSEL Master Scenario Events List.

performance of both basic and routine tasks as well as more complex and ambiguous issues. Most often, taskers and injects are scattered throughout the exercise and timed for release into the exercise by controllers who carefully monitor what emergency workers are doing. The basic differentiation is that taskers most often levy new requirements and assignments on players while injects offer a new set of facts, a new problem, or a novel situation that must be dealt with in the midst of the crisis itself. Exercise designers must think carefully about including realistic taskers and injects that could actually occur during deployed crisis operations and avoid inserting extraneous or frivolous problems into the exercises that may actually detract first responders from doing their job. Distractions and unexpected obstacles can be inserted as further problems in an exercise as long as the overall effort and purpose is balanced and realistic. Examples could include impromptu media incursions, reports of missing persons in the crisis area, discovery of new hazmat explosives in the crisis area or other events that are relevant and realistic.

The *eighth design step* requires that exercise planners and designers devise metrics and expected outcomes for each tasker and inject that allow evaluators, trainees, political officials, and other observers to see how assigned and unfolding taskers will be handled. This will require not only a decision to time the tasker in the flow of ordinary exercise events, but also to determine if the tasker is actually a distraction, disrupter, or delaying element in the overall disaster scenario itself. For example, while first responders are working on all the aspects of a six-alarm fire in a chemical storage facility, an unexpected 80 mph wind shear or tornado comes within a half mile of the emergency, triggering some significant on-the-spot decisions by the EOC and incident commander about how to handle the new threat or emergency situation. Another variation would have seven emergency responders trapped inside the burning

TIME	EVENT	Task Assigned	Expected Actions
======	=======	===============	==================
08:33	Explosion Reported At Archives Metro Station by Station Manager	Specify Unit--Function	1—dispatch 911 2—assemble units 3—identify injuries 4—identify damages 5—specify if CBRN?? 6—Identify trains affected 7—estimate response package

Figure 2.4

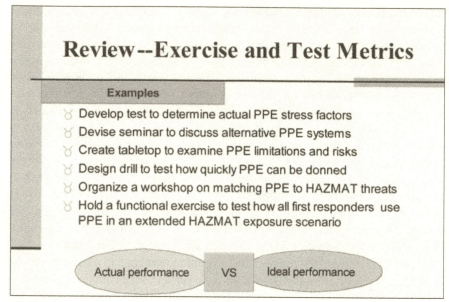

Figure 2.5   Review—Exercise and Test Metrics.

warehouse while the flames appear to be closing in on the more explosive and toxic chemicals stored inside the building. This triggers a need for adjusting the overall response strategy to deal with the new emergency. Testing the metrics enables a revalidation of key tasks and activities deemed essential to effective emergency response and permits both players and observers to calibrate their performance against objective measures of high-quality behavior.

Remember, expected outcomes detailed on MSEL sheets do several important things crucial to the exercise: (1) identify ideal responder behavior, (2) specify actions to be taken and often in what sequence, (3) illustrate what key communication and further tasking may be required, and (4) reveal elements of a decision that players and emergency managers must complete before executing further relevant activities. In this way, expected outcomes provide key guidance for exercise evaluators.

While more details will be provided later, the overall cast of characters involved in exercise design and development include the following people who normally work on the task of exercise design and development at a *ratio of four design weeks to each full day of exercise content.*

Exercise Design & Development Staff

1. Controller
2. Designer and/or Coordinator of support staff

3. Support staff (MSEL writers, response cell staff, logistics, communications and administrative staff)
4. Experts and advisors (security staff and transportation assistants)
5. Evaluators and Observers

The *ninth step* requires some careful consideration of how certain ongoing and complex tasks that will likely cover several hours or days to complete can be simulated so that these difficult-to-conclude tasks and challenges are incorporated into the exercise. Here the examination of alternative message options and the design of the exercise management structure could produce outcomes where emergency responders must consider a *stop action* in the exercise itself to discuss how they would bring a particular problem under control or whether they would expect the state or federal officials involved to assume responsibility for disposing of additional emergency burdens.

Examples would include the actual decontamination of a highly contaminated area adjacent to a school or business and how that project would be completed apart from final resolution of the explosion or toxic disaster itself. Here, the emphasis is on follow-on activities deemed essential to recovery, cleanup or other tasks designed to render safe a previously dangerous area and keep the area secure from public interference or encroachment until professional experts have determined that specific area is now safe. This is an optional area of activity but could be essential in further technical or operational training if emergency responders are unfamiliar with the set of technical or related downstream issues involved.

The *tenth step* simply requires that all exercise evaluators and designated observers compile their respective notes and observations, including interviews with key players and expert observers, to enable an overall assessment of the exercise to be drafted. This step assumes that certain evaluation criteria in addition to the specified performance metrics developed in *step 8* have been sufficiently articulated such that more specific determinations can be made about how certain exercise problems and special challenges were handled by the emergency responders playing in the exercise. Evaluators should discuss their preliminary findings with exercise designers and controllers, making sure that major issues and exercise objectives have been addressed adequately. More formal and deeply analytical aspects will be covered in a final evaluation report that is shared with emergency responders and managers who actually played in the exercise. This should be done within six weeks of the exercise completion to further reinforce any learning or special insights that designers and controllers wanted to impart.

Finally the *eleventh and last step* involves a hotwash, which is an unstructured but largely guided discussion led by a combination of exercise designers and evaluators. Some of these hotwashes can go on for hours but the most effective length seems to be usually sixty to ninety minutes. The overall goal of the hotwash is to afford all exercise participants the opportunity to share their own perspectives about what went smoothly, where there were gaps and problems and what insights were derived from the event. Here the objective is clearly not to assign blame or suggest poor performance but instead focus on areas of improvement and aspects of overall exercise conduct where remedial steps seem sensible and warranted. It comes at the end of the exercise involving designers, controllers, response cell, staff, observers, and emergency responders who played in the exercise. The primary overall aim is to bring out the three or four major findings or issues that evaluators and exercise controllers felt were accomplished or revealed by the exercise. The hotwash also allows players to express and vent their own feelings about what operational issues and problems merit attention.

The second chief aim is to solicit and capture the views, opinions, and perspectives of those playing within the exercise itself to allow them an opportunity to express their ideas, concerns, and experiences. This is an especially crucial time to gather information from players about whether they thought the scenario, taskers, and other exercise events were both challenging and realistic. They should also be told during the hotwash that within six weeks an *After-Action Report* (AAR) will be completed that summarizes the exercise and highlights the major insights and lessons gathered from the exercise experience. Sometimes minority views and perspectives included in an AAR will help illustrate fair and justifiable differences of opinion about what happened and why certain outcomes turned out the way they did. Fairness, objectivity and targeted commentary are the key aspects of an AAR.

This final step allows all people involved to know how the entire exercise process comes full circle from its beginnings in design to the issuance of the AAR. The AAR will identify strengths, weaknesses, shortfalls, and successes, also underscoring opportunities for further training and areas where further staff development and performance may need to be upgraded. There is no doubt that sometimes an AAR will be used to ruthlessly cut staff or budgets, streamline or curtail certain functions, or create an excuse to terminate a supervisor or key person. That is not the main purpose of an AAR, but the political pressures that may be applied mean AAR authors must be vigilant about the language involved. In completing these ten crucial steps and retaining the documentation for future reference, all insights and valuable observations can be used by others to refine and improve emergency operations long after the exercise ends. Of course, another advantage of the hotwash is that it allows players to decompress and return to their normal state of behavior and settled emotions, which is important if the stressful realism of an exercise brought many players into a strained emotional environment.

DISCUSSION QUESTIONS

1. What is the most important issue to test in exercise design?
2. Why should exercise designs include several different taskers?
3. What matters most in the first three steps of exercise design?
4. How would the first page of an MSEL look for the first two hours of the exercise?
5. What is an AAR designed to do? How does a hotwash help evaluators?
6. What should be done with the results of a hotwash?

YOU TRY IT—RESEARCH TASKS

1. Write a draft exercise scenario dealing with a significant natural disaster.
2. What metrics would you develop for a complex hazmat exercise? Why?
3. What key performance issues would you like to test and exercise?
4. What training or guidance should evaluators get?
5. What constitutes "great performance" in a capabilities-based exercise involving a hasty flood rescue at a nursing home?

NOTES

1. EMERGENCY SUPPORT FUNCTION ANNEXES: INTRODUCTION. Purpose. This section provides an overview of the Emergency Support Function (ESF) www.fema.gov/pdf/emergency/nrf/nrf-esf-intro.pdf; also see National Response Framework and TCL which defines 37 specific capabilities, www.dhs.gov/xlibrary/assets/National_Preparedness_Guidelines.pdf (Accessed September 13, 2007).
2. Lessons Learned Information Sharing (LLIS.gov) Lessons Learned and Best Practices for emergency response providers. https://www.llis.dhs.gov.
3. NFPA 300 consensus codes and standards intended to minimize the possibility and effects of fire and other disasters. www.nfpa.org/displayContent.asp?categoryID.

Chapter 3

Issues in Exercise Design

There are several significant issues that exercise designers should seriously consider when compiling the elements of a draft exercise design and strategy. Designers must face the possibility that they cannot assemble the talent, time, or technical expertise needed to structure and conduct a realistic exercise, but they must be committed nonetheless to trying alternatives that demonstrate the exemplars of readiness that they seek to illustrate. Strapped for resources, short of key personnel or equipment, or facing an exercise design event that political leaders are not inclined to support may reflect the reality some emergency managers face. Nevertheless, they must ponder which alternative approach to exercise design best fits the situation confronting them. Among those basic and fundamental considerations are the issues outlined below.

- What type of exercise is best given our situation?
- Can we realistically replicate the demands and risks of a crisis environment?
- Should we hire an expert to design an exercise?
- What are the expected costs of exercise design?
- What are the most important tasks and functions to exercise?
- Should we approach a local university for assistance in design?
- Should we borrow the exercise design of another city or town?
- Should we control our scarce resources and join with other communities?

Of course, these are not exhaustive of all the questions and concerns a city or community may have in designing an exercise, but they raise important issues that should be addressed. In many jurisdictions, the question of emergency exercise design will likely fall on the emergency manager who must worry about getting full participation and involvement from all those key persons and organizations whose involvement makes the exercise believable and realistic. This completely undermines the manager's central role as overall coordinator of first responders and exempts the manager from playing with his staff. Securing outside talent from professional associations, retired emergency managers, or hired expertise is essential to the design task. If certain key personnel or institutions cannot or will not participate, arrangements must be made to insert a different scenario or simulate their active involvement with a credible substitute.

One key issue that exercise designers must wrestle with early in the design process is the question of selecting the best exercise vehicle for demonstrating that first responders, EOC personnel, and support staff have the requisite training and experience to successfully and effectively handle the wide array of issues they could confront. If you consider for a moment *the different target capabilities that DHS says major cities and jurisdictions must wrestle with, let alone the different response capabilities that appear to be the fundamental ones stressed for overall readiness*, we see that exercises can range from discussion seminars and tabletop exercises to fully deployed and sophisticated functional exercises where multiple jurisdictions and federal and state players are intricately involved in the exercise.

Becoming aware of the *TCL—Target Capabilities List*—that DHS has published will help in articulating some of the exercise tasks essential to demonstrating preparedness. Knowing the full spectrum of exercise options is very important and research has shown that the most time-saving and cost-effective approach is the tabletop exercises (TTX). The general advisory warning is that TTX events are less complicated and do not require a "full rollout" of personnel, equipment, and special logistics or communications that would ordinarily be required in a full-scale or deployed exercise. The main issue is to understand the different kinds of exercise options and then select the right one to fit the situation.

In a similar vein, exercises designed to deal with NIMS, NIPP, ESF and related issues which deal with operational and functional matters at a deeper and more finite level of granularity deserve careful thought. Here the emphasis is not only on how your own community's array of emergency response personnel and equipment might perform but how their efforts would integrate with state, federal, military and business interests and activities intended to align and support what needs to be done. Coordinated tasks and orchestrated operational matters at this juncture are more important to test, assess, and validate.

It makes sense to choose the right exercise, which fits the budget, objectives, and needs of the community. Some approaches are better suited for the situation than others, and in some cases you may want participation by local citizens or the private sector to replicate what these entities may actually do given the exercise scenario and demands placed on them by the crisis.

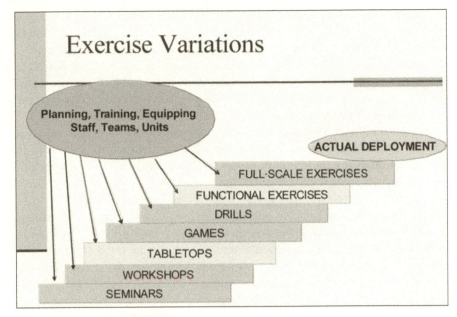

Figure 3.1 Exercise Variations

Table 3.1 Exercise Options: Advantages and Disadvantages

Exercise Type	Advantages	Disadvantages
Seminars	easy and cheap	limited test of readiness
Workshops	simple well focused	no significant stresses
Tabletops	brings key leaders together	no test of capability
Games	replicates major issues	rush for easy answers
Drills	rigid test of preparedness	may not test all aspects
Functional Exercise	realistic test of readiness	expensive, complicated
Full-Scale Exercise	every key function tested	never enough time

In most cases, exercise selection will be driven by available budget, resources, personnel, and opportunities to demonstrate how responders and equipment function together. Testing capabilities and overcoming performance gaps are key.

Exercise options have their strengths and weaknesses, which are influenced by many factors as outlined in Table 3.1.

The first and foremost issue in any exercise design situation is the objectives—what do we want the exercise to reveal or demonstrate? Proving hazmat-response capability is one thing, and testing emergency response team problem solving in a unique crisis is quite another. Settling on coherent and measurable objectives will be the first and most crucial set of questions that exercise designers must address. When building an MSEL it is especially important to identify the major tasks, activities, and operations that exercise designers and controllers expect to see performed and completed on an hour-by-hour basis. These objective requirements provide the backbone of the exercise and form the central analytical theme of exercise evaluations. It cannot be stressed enough that objectives that outline the principal tasks, activities, and operations expected during an exercise drive the entire enterprise itself, making it nearly impossible to structure a coherent and effective exercise at all if objectives are ill conceived, incomplete, or faulty.

In addition, exercise designers need to examine how the people involved in the actual exercises may perform and what special requirements may be placed on them for the duration of the exercises. This should be carefully thought out and planned in advance.

We must determine what players will be doing, what observers will be allowed to do so that exercise objectives and realism are not sacrificed, and finally what exercise facilitators ought to be doing. In some cases facilitators will be called controllers or coordinators to distinguish them from exercise managers and evaluators. These distinctions will be discussed later. Evaluators should be separated from others in the exercise because they must have the ability to move anywhere and observe any action, interview any player,

Exercise Design Objectives (Major University—Urban Setting)

Exercise design objectives focus on improving understanding of a response concept, identifying opportunities or problems, and achieving a change in attitude. Exercises must focus on the following design objectives identified by the Exercise Planning Team:

1. Identification and Notification. Determine response capabilities for arriving on-scene, determining a toxic material has been released, and making proper notification.
2. Campus Response. Assess the actions of campus security to warn the campus community and follow Emergency Operations Plans (EOPs) for responding to a hazardous release.
3. Incident Command Structure. Emphasize the ICS and how all agencies will work in an integrated and supportive manner throughout incident.
4. Public Information. Address methods for providing timely and accurate information, released from one source to inform the public and minimize the chaos.
5. Supportive Roles. Enlist the assistance of key campus administrators and other college personnel for response and recovery issues.
6. Medical Capabilities. Determine the capacity of community medical facilities to manage mass casualty situations pertaining to chemical exposure.

and examine any materials related to the effective performance of tasks and activities. Evaluators will also listen to hotwash comments and review reports and interview materials from key players because the evaluators will often become the principal authors of the exercise After-Action Report (AAR).

Beginning with the basic elements, let's examine how the outlines and structure of a small-scale emergency plan and its essential parts may fit together into a coherent pattern that reflects some of the key considerations that help support and sustain a valid exercise plan. We will start with *assumptions and artificialities*, which will help determine the scope and duration of the exercise. Of course, we have tucked away our preliminary exercise objectives for now to ensure we have examined these basic considerations. In any exercise, assumptions and artificialities may be necessary to complete play in the time allotted. For example, during this TTX exercise, the following assumptions and artificialities provide the basic ingredients necessary to keep the overall structure and theme as simple as possible. Here are some examples:

- The scenario is plausible, and events occur as they are presented.
- There is no hidden agenda, and there are *no trick questions*.

Exercise Participants

- Players. Players respond to the situation presented based on expert knowledge of response procedures, current plans and procedures, and insights derived from training.
- Observers. Observers support the group in developing responses to the situation during the discussion; they are not participants in the moderated discussion period, however.
- Facilitators. Facilitators provide situation updates and moderate discussions. They also provide additional information or resolve questions as required. Key Exercise Planning Team members also may assist with facilitation as subject matter experts (SMEs) during the TTX. These people may also be called controllers or coordinators, depending upon the identification scheme that the exercise designers select.
- Evaluators. Observe, review, and monitor exercise activities to determine if taskers were handled in a complete and timely manner, whether unique or unexpected problems were tackled effectively, and how crisis communications were handled at every key step of the exercise. Evaluators will also assess the performance and operation of special equipment and determine whether emergency responders displayed a professional level of training in doing their jobs.

- All players receive information at the same time.
- Existence of special technologies and equipment is assumed to be available.
- Exercise assumes players have a level of training equivalent to two years experience.
- Exercise time is arranged so one exercise hour equals four real hours.
- All players have access to the same information and EOP guidance.
- Exercise controllers have agreed the game will last less than six hours.

We will select a simple exercise structure for the TTX that features a scenario, an MSEL, sequential taskers, criteria for evaluation, and other material considered useful. The overall exercise schedule and design principles call for only two modules, which will be gradually introduced to the test by the emergency response team using a deliberate scenario. Participants will then address the following sequence of basic modules:

- Module 1: Incident Notification
- Module 2: Response

Each module begins with an update that summarizes key events occurring within that time period. After the updates, participants review the situation and engage in functional group discussions of appropriate response issues. The scenario calls for assessing incident notification and initial emergency response to a hazmat trailer-tanker spill adjacent to a community college campus. As such, the functional groups to be exercised and affected are as follows:

- Campus security/law enforcement
- Fire/hazardous materials (hazmat) local jurisdiction
- Hospital/EMS (emergency medical services)
- Campus president's office/administration
- Emergency manager (community college)
- Public information/media

At the end of six hours of combined tasker-led assignments and free-play problems designed to assess emergency response readiness, these functional groups engage in post-exercise hotwash discussions. Immediately thereafter, participants will engage in a facilitated caucus discussion in which a spokesperson from each group will present a synopsis of the group's actions, based on the scenario. The overall aim of the exercise includes several related objectives:

1. test first responders control of a hazmat event with minimal injuries
2. test on campus alert, warning systems, and interagency communications
3. test performance of campus police

4. test on-campus triage and emergency transit procedures
5. test public information capabilities and performance

In a TTX it is assumed that a secure area with phones, computers, note-pads, work areas, maps, highway diagrams, building schematics, technical reference guides and other relevant reference material is on hand. It is usually best to do the TTX adjacent to the Emergency Ops Center where the exercise is being conducted and assemble the players, controllers, evaluators at least *thirty* minutes prior to the TTX to review the day's events and outline overall requirements. In some cases, nonessential and superfluous or frivolous taskers and injects make sense because they can throw players off track. They should be kept to a minimum. Now let's look at a sample tabletop exercise (TTX) and examine the sequence of events that depict the emergency situation which all TTX players must address.

SAMPLE SCENARIO

Bixby Community College (BCC), founded in 1960, is a community college on Florida's western panhandle coast approximately fifteen miles from Pensacola adjacent to the smaller fire departments of Milton and Pace. The Pensacola Campus is home to approximately 2,000 non-residential students, 89 full and part-time staff, 53 full-time faculty, and 93 adjunct faculty. This picturesque campus with sizeable lake and wooded surroundings is situated on 150 acres between state road 90 and I-10. There are five buildings (administrative and classroom), an aquatic center, day care, softball field and expansive parking areas. Looking south from the buildings is Interstate 10 which is parallel to the campus and within 100 yards of the main parking area. Secondary roads flank two sides of the campus while lakes and wooded wetlands make up the remaining circumference.

BCC maintains an unarmed security department on each campus led by a security coordinator. The main campus is supported by its own police department consisting of eight officers and three vehicles. Pensacola Fire & Rescue and Pensacola Regional Hospital are about thirteen miles west of campus. Santa Rosa County Emergency Operations Center in Pace, located approximately twelve miles west of campus is staffed by six full-time employees and many volunteers. It is a modern facility with appropriate equipment and space to manage a wide range of emergencies or disasters. However, it is not as fully resourced as Escambia County's EOC. BCC's security department is well supported by the campus president and dean of students, who believe in comprehensive and integrated planning and training with the local response community and business community.

Module 1: Incident Notification

Day 1: 0950

BCC has a full schedule of classes this morning beginning at 0800 and students are still trying to find parking spaces while others are hurrying across the lot. It is an overcast day with off-shore winds ranging from 5 to 10 mph. Suddenly, the morning routine is interrupted by the high-pitched screeching of breaks and the inevitable sound of a high-impact collision.

Day 1: 0951

Officer Bushnell of the campus Security Department is monitoring the parking situation from his golf cart in the main lot of the campus. He hears the sound of the crash and turns to observe an overturned tanker truck with smoke billowing from around the cabin area. He immediately engages his radio and notifies dispatch of the accident instructing them to contact 911. He indicates that a tanker was traveling eastbound on I-10 adjacent to the campus and it appears another vehicle was involved. Fire and black smoke are present and billowing over the parking lot.

Day 1: 0953

The 911 call center is inundated with phone calls from travelers calling on cell phones to report the accident. Sources indicated that a northbound vehicle crossed the median and collided head-on with the tanker creating a multi-vehicle crash. Some reports say that there appears to be a substance leaking from the tank. Dispatch is contacting Pensacola Fire and Rescue, BCC police, Santa Rosa County EOC, Escambia County Hazmat, and state officials in Tallahassee.

Day 1: 1005

Santa Rosa County Fire and Rescue, along with three trucks from nearby Pensacola, are now on-scene and from a distance of approximately a half mile detects the smell of chlorine. This is further confirmed by the visible placards on the vehicle observed through binoculars. Based on this information, they notify dispatch to send a hazmat unit to the scene.

Day 1: 1008

Florida Highway Patrol (FHP) arrives on scene to assess the situation and control traffic, which has been stopped in both the northbound and southbound directions. Preliminary estimates of casualties are three dead, seven injured, nearby homes and businesses at risk. The medical examiner's office is notified and autopsy processing is initiated.

Day 1: 1011

Students on BCC campus are starting to feel the effects of an exposure to a noxious chemical, exhibiting signs and symptoms including coughing; choking; shortness of breath; and burning sensation in their eyes, nose, and throat.

Day 1: 1023

BCC's campus notifies the Santa Rosa County Fire dispatch of the symptoms their students and staff are exhibiting and requests the response of medical aid. At least eight students have collapsed complaining of toxic gas symptoms.

Day 1: 1026

Local television and radio stations interrupt their regular morning programming with news of the accident. Crews have been dispatched to the scene and begin arriving, asking for information. There are few details provided other than there was an accident on I-10 involving a truck carrying hazardous materials, which is releasing a chemical that appears to be affecting the BCC campus.

Day 1: 1027

BCC activates its EOP calling for sheltering all students in place currently inside the buildings due to the perceived threat of a poisonous gas, with a preliminary identification of chlorine. This involves moving all building occupants to the upper floors of the buildings.

Key Issues

- An accident involving a truck carrying hazardous materials has occurred on the interstate corridor adjacent to the community college impacting its students.
- On-scene responders have identified the leaking material.
- News crews are arriving on the scene and asking for updates.
- Students are affected and are exhibiting signs and symptoms of exposure.
- The community college activates its emergency plan based on information provided by local responders.

Questions

Based on the information provided, identify any additional requirements, critical issues, decisions, or questions that should be addressed at this time.

The following questions are provided as suggested general subjects that you may wish to address as the discussion progresses. These questions are not meant to constitute a definitive list of concerns to be addressed, nor is there a requirement to address every question.

Law Enforcement/BCC Security

1. At this stage of the response, what is the role of local/state law enforcement? BCC security?
2. What other actions would you take at this point? Why?
3. What, if any, additional local resources would you request at this time? How?
4. What are your perimeter and security concerns? How will these concerns be addressed? What steps will be taken and what resources will be required?
5. What are your primary safety concerns for your personnel? What steps should be taken to address these safety concerns? What resources may be required?
6. What are your priority action items at this point in the response?

Campus President's Office/Administration

1. At this point in the response, what notification would have been made, and by whom? How would local agencies be notified of the situation? What steps would be taken to notify faculty and students?
2. What Mutual Aid Agreements (MAAs) or Memorandums of Understanding (MOUs) do you currently have in place that could be used for this response? Would mutual aid be requested at this point? If so, from whom?
3. Would county Emergency Operations Center (EOC) be activated? If so, what is the activation process and how long would it take? How would these various entities communicate?
4. What are your primary concerns for students and campus first responders? What steps should be taken to address these safety concerns? What resources may be required?
5. Who has the authority to order an evacuation or shelter in place?

Fire/Hazmat

1. What other actions should you take at this point?
2. At this point, what information does the public need to have? How should this information be provided to them?

3. What additional resources would you need at this point?
4. What is your primary concern for your personnel? How will these concerns be addressed? What steps will be taken, and what resources will be required?
5. What are your priority action items at this point?

Hospital/EMS

1. Would the local hospital be notified of the incident at this point? If so, who would be responsible for making the notification?
2. Who is responsible for decontamination of victims before transporting them to the local area hospital?
3. Are the local EMS assets enough to handle a multi-casualty incident such as this? If not, have additional assets been identified? Are MOUs or MSSs in place?

Emergency Management

1. Would Escambia County EOC be activated at this time? What is the evacuation process for local homes and businesses, and how long would it take? How would these various entities communicate? Who has the responsibility to order the evacuation?
2. Are personnel identified to staff the EOC? How long will it take to be fully operational?
3. What are your priority actions at this time?

Public Information/Media

1. Who would be the Public Information Officer (PIO) for BCC?
2. What other agency PIOs would be contributing?
3. With a multitude of agencies becoming involved in the response, how would you coordinate information among the various PIOs? Would a single PIO for the whole incident be identified? Is so, who would be a likely candidate?
4. Would there be a pre-designated site for media staging and press conferences? Is this needed? Where would a likely location be?
5. What is the current plan or strategy for providing information to the media and the public?
6. At this point, what information does the public need to have? How should this information be disseminated to them? Who should be the primary spokesperson for this event? How often should public updates be provided?

Module 2: Response

Day 1: 0958

First arriving emergency response units from Santa Rosa County Fire and Rescue set up an initial isolation zone around the leaking tanker and attempt to address fire concerns. FHP initiates their traffic contingency plan for shutting down the interstate and rerouting traffic onto local streets. State roads 87, 89, and 90 are affected. SW winds are 30 mph.

Day 1: 0959

College security personnel initiate their emergency plan and start notification up the chain of command to the college administration. Plans to shelter in place all building occupants already on campus are put into place.

Day 1: 1002

Santa Rosa and Escambia County EOCs are activated for a multi-casualty incident affecting the community college. Notifications are made to local and state officials.

Day 1: 1008

Local EOC personnel are in contact with college authorities to coordinate the actions of local agencies and deployment of assets in response to the events on BCC's campus.

Day 1: 1012

Local law enforcement is struggling to establish and maintain a secure perimeter in the face of an increasing crowd of onlookers, which now includes television news crews. Access routes to the scene must be kept open for emergency responders, but the roadways are filling with people as well as vehicle traffic. Although many people in the area have already started to self-evacuate, the incident commander officially requests an evacuation of the section of the city downwind of the accident site.

Day 1: 1014

The evacuation ordered by the incident commander is revised to shelter in place all people who are in public buildings within the evacuation zone. He also advises the shutting down of all HVAC systems, closing of all windows and doors, and the movement of personnel to upper floors. The BCC campus is especially vulnerable, as perhaps 1,200 students are on campus and another 200 are en route to the campus.

Day 1: 1015

College security personnel receive information from Escambia County Hazmat Team on-scene through the EOC that the chemical has been identified and personnel and students sheltered in place should be moved to upper floors due to the properties of the toxic material being released. They also advise warning students en route to stay away from campus until they hear an "all-clear" on the radio or TV.

Day 1: 1016

The roads are becoming gridlocked as people are trying to leave the area, complicated by the students arriving for morning classes. Additional assets from local law enforcement are requested to combat this mounting problem.

Day 1: 1022

Campus security has fully implemented their EOP and activated their accountability system. A notification has been made to the incident command post requesting EMS support for students exhibiting signs and symptoms of chemical exposure.

Day 1: 1026

Several students are transported to the local hospital for evaluation, though all injuries seem to be minor. Accountability is difficult as BCC is a community college with no resident students on campus. Staff has been accounted for and no report of injuries has been reported by anyone among them.

Day 1: 1055

The Escambia County Hazmat team has controlled the leaking tanker and the release of the chlorine has stopped. A notification to the EOC is made and the evacuation order is lifted allowing people to return to their homes in the affected area.

Day 1: 1105

The campus administration is notified of the status of the incident and told to lift the shelter-in-place order at their location. Notifications are made down through the command structure to the security personnel who begin telling students to report back to their classrooms.

Day 1: 1125

Local area hospital reports a total of twenty-eight transported casualties with ten admissions for acute symptoms. Although taxed, the hospital retains normal operations in their emergency room.

Day 1: 1144

Escambia County and Santa Rosa County EOC is stood down as the incident is terminated. BCC campus police review their on-campus situation and search for any missing students or faculty.

Summary of Casualties

Day 1: 1250

Estimated casualties thirty-five to thirty-nine (twenty-eight on campus—nine proximate to spill)
Estimated fatalities three (two more in critical condition)

Key Issues

- Local hospitals, while overwhelmed by the number of victims who require treatment, continued to operate. Examine how they handled the surge!
- The incident has been determined to be an accident.
- The public and media need to be supplied with accurate and helpful information to reduce confusion and panic and promote safety and confidence.
- The campus emergency response system functioned properly with minor deficiencies throughout the incident.

Questions

Based on the information provided, participate in the discussion concerning the issues raised in Module 2. Identify any additional requirements, critical issues, decisions, or questions that should be addressed at this time.

The following questions are provided as suggested general subjects that you may wish to address as the discussion progresses. These questions are not meant to constitute a definitive list of concerns to be addressed, nor is there a requirement to address every question in this section.

Law Enforcement/BCC Security

1. What are your perimeter, security, and traffic concerns at this point in the incident?
2. What role does your agency have in facilitating an orderly evacuation of the area or campus population? What actions could be taken to improve the current situation and ensure that all responders have access to the site and that EMS has an unobstructed path to area hospitals?

3. Would the release of a different hazardous material alter your EOP?
4. What does the activation of the local EOC mean to your agency?
5. What are your priority action items for consideration at this point in the incident?

Fire/Hazmat

1. How would the arrival of additional external resources, such as the Navy's EM Response force from the nearby military base, or the state's hazmat response team, change your incident command/command and control structure? How would these additional resources be integrated into the response effort? Who commands them?
2. What challenges were being faced before the hazmat team arrived on-scene? Where would assets be staged for this incident? Are the communications and equipment interoperable and interchangeable?
3. Would tactics change based on weather conditions? If a wind shift or other change occurred during the incident, which affected your tactics, how would that information be communicated to the other response agencies?
4. What does the activation of the EOC mean to your team?
5. What are your priority action items for consideration at this point in the incident?

Emergency Manager

1. How is the EOC staffed at this point in the incident? What preparations would be made to staff for a possible extended activation? Are the current staffing protocols sufficient to support extended activation? If not, how might this situation be remedied? Who would be the PIO for BCC?
2. What is the public relations strategy at this point? Would you predesignate a site for the press conferences? Where? What specific information should be provided at this time? What information should not be disclosed? How will this be coordinated with on-scene incident personnel?
3. What are the priority action items for consideration at this point for the EOC?
4. Are state resources required? What is the process for obtaining them?

Campus President's Office/Administration

1. Who would be the PIO for BCC? Would the campus president or a representative from that office make a statement to the media? Why or why not?
2. Would campus administration personnel be a part of a unified command structure if one were established?

3. Does the campus have adequate assets to address a prolonged need to shelter in place? What needs to be addressed?
4. Does BCC police have a representative at the EOC? How would information be coordinated from the EOC back to the campus and to whom?
5. Did the pre-incident planning for an event of this magnitude work? What deficiencies were identified and what steps can be taken to address them?

Public Information/Media

1. What specific information about the incident would you release at this time to the media for dissemination to the public? What topics should be covered and what information should not be disclosed? Why?
2. Media personnel are at local hospitals, the Escambia EOC, BCC campus and various other locations. How can incident PIOs manage the information being disseminated?
3. How can the media be used as an effective tool in disseminating information to the public?
4. What information/direction might be useful for the public/college community to know following this event?

Hospital/EMS

1. Are the local area hospitals equipped to handle contaminated patients? If not, have alternate means for decontamination been identified and addressed?
2. What notifications were made prior to the hospitals receiving patients if any? Who made those notifications?
3. Did the emergency room of the local area ever become overwhelmed at any time, causing them to turn away routine emergency walk-ins?
4. Did EMS have enough assets to handle all of the transport patients? Were there contingency plans in place if there were more victims? How was the surge handled?
5. Were any of the EMS workers or transport vehicles contaminated during the incident? If so, how was this addressed?
6. How many walking wounded presented for treatment?

TABLETOP TRAINING ANNEX

This exercise example of a TTX is intended to illustrate in general terms the kinds of specific activities and functional response areas that would normally be tested in a tabletop exercise where the key players who represent BCC and county personnel could discuss each problem and their response to it, eventually settling on either confirmation of well-known solutions or aggregate strategies to handle similar problems if they were to arise in the future. In addition, colleges are wonderful locations to use as a test-bed examining best practices, training techniques, technologies, and projected solutions to emergency problems where the combined expertise of faculty, practitioners, business experts, citizens, media, and others can usefully contribute to a better understanding of emergency management issues. Better yet, the campus can provide a training site for simulating EOC operations and serve as a standby EOC in the event that the original one falls victim to a disaster and is rendered inoperable.

Campus security officials and exercise planners should pay particular attention to the special constraints and circumstances that affect college campuses and their surrounding communities. Becoming aware of what colleges are capable of doing for themselves and knowing what impact local community emergency resources have at their disposal is crucial. Consequently, it is dangerous to make false assumptions about what the college can do or what the neighboring community can do unless meaningful discussions and exercises explore that set of issues.[1]

Testing the EOC itself is an important issue that requires some thoughtful assessment in planning what the various situations, problems, and demands

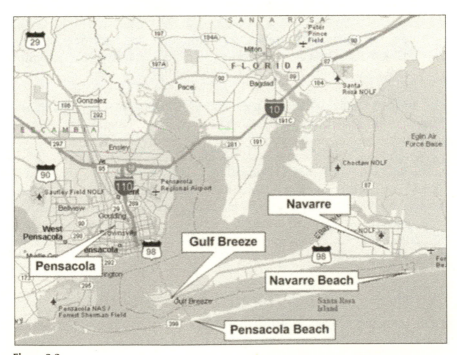

Figure 3.2

could be in an emergency. Just testing the sheer functionality of the EOC is also worth considering, as often people make the dangerous assumption that "all is well" and never test the underlying elements and system that make an EOC viable. Here is a partial list, taken from DHS, which outlines some of the principal test and exercise areas that should be examined in looking at EOC functions and operations.

DHS Target Capabilities List (TCL)—Full Spectrum of EOC Management Includes:

- EOC activation, notification, staffing, and deactivation
- Management, direction, control, and coordination of response and recovery activities
- Coordination of efforts among neighboring governments at each level and among local, regional, state, and federal EOCs
- Coordination of public information and warning
- Maintenance of the information and communication necessary for coordinating response and recovery activities
- Survey of target organization, risk zones, and hazard domains
- Identify NIMS, NFPA, other requirements for personnel and equipment
- Specify performance metrics for hazmat and special emergency technologies

Again, the focus of exercises is to pinpoint the specific function, task, or activity that you want to test and make certain your assumptions about emergency responder training and preparedness are correct. These aspects must be verified through exercises unless one accepts the risk that at any given time unexercised elements of your emergency response force will not behave as effectively and comprehensively as they would if they were properly trained and exercised. This means a purposeful and sometimes tedious review of basic emergency functions, tasks, and activities to assure yourself—especially if you are the emergency manager—that all systems, personnel, and their equipment are ready for almost any kind of "all-hazard" scenario. To do otherwise is to delude oneself, mislead the public, and undermine the esprit de corps of your emergency first responders. Here is a brief example for review and reinforcement.

Example

Draft goal: Test activation of the county emergency notification system for tornados and EOC operations during first sixty minutes.

Potential Specific Objectives

Test activation of the county emergency notification system through a table-top workshop of emergency managers and citizen leaders to assess the system's effectiveness.

Scenario

Issue a countywide emergency warning related to a tornado threat that may affect the county, involving at least three different communities, three schools, four factories, and a nursing home. Exercise should test formulation, delivery, receipt, and understanding of the warning message.

MSEL Factors

Task players to develop a warning message, simulate delivery of the message, discuss with citizen volunteers message understanding and receipt. Verify if all would take directed precautionary actions for their safety.

Testing interrelationships and interdependencies and coordinating arrangements and communication protocols are all part of an EOC exercise focus.

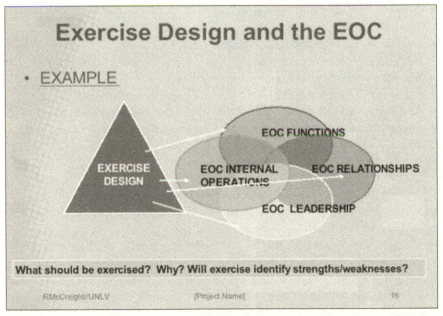

Figure 3.3   EOC staff must be exercised independently of Incident Command to test their respective communications, procedures, staffing and message management and to ensure proper coordination and collaboration schemes are working as planned.

EOC leadership must be tested and all of its vertical, horizontal, and unique connections to federal, state, NGO, and private sector organizations should be examined. Nothing should be taken for granted, as this is the command post for emergency operations and its *linkage to the on-scene incident commander is crucial.*

Certainly we understand by now that systematic testing and refining of EOC capabilities enables a firmer and more complete *understanding of emergency readiness* than anyone would have without the exercise experience behind them. Keep the essential design requirements simple and straightforward as you design TTXs and check periodically to see if you have accounted for realistic constraints, demands, and setbacks in your scenario and MSEL plan. Below is a quick review of essential design elements.

ESSENTIAL DESIGN ELEMENTS

- Scenario (objectives/assumptions/artificialities—task orientation)
- Controllers-evaluators (handbooks-SOPs)
- Badging—access/restrictions on players/evaluators/controllers
- Safety, security, and logistics (real-time standby resources)
- Computer support and communications
- Table of MSELs, injects, and freeplay options
- Evaluation plan (interviews/observation/CCTV?) AARs?
- Real-time versus exercise time (7/24 or staged days of exercise work)
- Site map/venue for play (actual vs. simulated)
- Event flow—task execution—stop-action procedures outlined
- Assigned roles (equipment and technology tests and demonstrations)
- Exercise schedule—scripted, freeplay, or phased movement?
- Event tracking/task completion/unfinished tasks/novel problems
- Media and public affairs (privacy—gag orders)

At this point, we have covered many of the basic elements and requirements for designing an exercise, even a modest and simple TTX, with due regard for the fact that no universal formula or cookbook approach is anointed as the only way to proceed. It is true that DHS has assembled the pilot HSEEP system to assist in many of these tasks but early information from state and local governments suggests they prefer something simple, understandable, and repeatable for their clients and first responders. It remains to be seen whether the years of experience in designing and conducting many state and local exercises can be meaningfully assembled, analyzed, and dissected to discern the most important issues and elements involved. This is one task for

[Exercise Design Objectives]
• Confirm individual/team training [KSA's]
• Demonstrate key performance functions
• Verify man-technology interface/operations
• Assess problem solving
• Examine response readiness metrics
• Observe extended/novel stress incidents
• Evaluate target capabilities
• Determine issues and areas for further tests

Figure 3.4   Exercise Design Objectives.

local colleges to perform in assisting their state and supporting their county to build a coherent and understandable database of best practices and exercise design insights. LLIS is also a useful resource.

By now you should have a collection of basic and essential elements in constructing an exercise. There is no substitute for doing the job, so it is highly recommended that you talk with experts, look at other exercise plans, and gather the best information possible before embarking on an exercise design project. However, it is reassuring to know that nothing in the entire exercise design project is beyond the scope or skill of any reader, and many in the emergency management business are eager to assist if necessary.

Exercise objectives should be simple, achievable, measurable, results oriented, observable, and valid. Only by practice and experience can one master the technique of writing good objectives. Figure 3.4 briefly reviews our main points covered in this chapter. (During earliest work to develop a graduate course on exercise design in 2009 I benefited from the opportunity to fine tune key ideas and concepts with contract teaching assignments at George Washington University and the University of Nevada where major principles were refined and identified.)

A key part of exercise design which is often overlooked is the relationship between information sharing and message management in the midst of a crisis. Exercise planners must consider the value of testing the assumptions and operations which undergird their information sharing strategies and provide an opportunity to test message management. See Appendix F for further details explaining this important issue.

QUESTIONS

1. What are the most important issues in exercise design? Why?
2. Which exercise design steps seem most challenging and complex? Why?
3. Why is it important to separately exercise the EOC?
4. What are the characteristics of a good tabletop exercise (TTX)? Why?

RESEARCH QUESTIONS

1. After reviewing your EOP what are the three most important emergency functions you would want to see exercised? Why? Does it seem clear that "shelter-in-place" is as well understood as "evacuation"? What specific events ought to trigger shelter-in-place?
2. What kind of TTX seems best to examine how local high school officials will respond to a serious hazmat emergency within a quarter mile of the school's athletic fields? Will you likely have to get parents and the school board involved in planning this exercise?
3. Think about a scenarios where augmentation and support from state and federal agencies might be required along with possible involvement of military support elements. This might entail a persistent toxic chemical release from a railcar spill that cannot be easily managed or controlled and employees as well active duty military personnel working at a nearby base within 3 miles of the community must respond and act because they are adversely affected by the incident. What special considerations should community leaders assess to maximize greatest possible coordination among these diverse organizations? explain your rationale.

NOTES

1. Report of the Virginia Tech Shooting—Review Panel. Available at: www.governor.virginia.gov Temp Content. Also see Georgetown University's Safety and Emergency Preparedness: http://www.georgetown.edu/campus-life/safety-and-emergency-preparedness/.

Chapter 4

Exercise Organization and Structure

We have established how important exercise objectives are for structuring the overall exercise, building the MSEL and outlining the specific taskers, activities, and operational behavior that comprise the skeleton of the exercise plan. In designing exercises, whether they are TTXs or full-scale deployed exercises spanning several days, the central challenge is to replicate as much realism as possible within the exercise itself so players can train, reinforce, and sharpen their emergency response skills. Players understand that certain assumptions and situational dynamics will require that certain exercise elements be simulated to a degree that precludes the replication of realistic emergency scenarios and that is understood for safety or security reasons to be prudent. For example, in testing hazmat training for a chlorine spill exercise, designers will likely use a stimulant that is noxious but not dangerous so firefighters and EMS staff can don their personal protective equipment (PPE) and deal with the emergency situation. However, if one wants to see how firefighters and others can actually function suited up in full protective gear, a controlled and safety-conscious replication of chlorine gas may be needed to see how the toxic environment actually affects responder performance.

The general rule is that exercise designers will want to create as realistic a training and test environment as can possibly be created. *However, if there is not due regard for safety in all aspects of the exercise involving the site, the equipment, and any technical risks that players may encounter, this will destroy the credibility and value of the exercise.* Without regard to the specific hazard circumstances, major urban areas should be testing themselves against the fifteen national planning scenarios (DHS) and each urban EM department should be annually evaluated on its performance in these different emergency situations. It makes sense that ten years after 9/11 we can create some useful benchmarks to calibrate how ready we really are. So in summary we are

asking that exercise designers build realism into exercises because they result
in better-prepared and ready emergency responders. More specifically, simulated activities and tasks should be designed to assess:

- functional responsibilities and key relationships
- target task completion
- logistical-technological resource dynamics
- communication patterns, flows and accountability
- problem solving and resolving unexpected situations
- overall readiness and preparedness
- whether significant vulnerabilities have been ameliorated
- successful emergency response performance (realistic metrics)
- media and public affairs (strategy, tactics, gag orders)

At the end of the periodic exercise process we are aiming to get better
information about our overall emergency response capability—our preparedness and readiness. Similarly, plans, training, equipment, doctrine and operational systems, and strategies must be periodically tested.

In many ways we are simply trying to validate our exercise plans, to validate the quality of prior emergency responder training and begin to ratchet
up our own standard of preparedness and readiness for the ultimate test—real
deployment to a real crisis. So we should take a closer look at the major structural aspects of exercise design—these are fundamental and crucial regardless
of whether the goal is to build a TTX or a full field-deployed exercise. Here
are the major structural elements:

- emergency plans
- exercise focus, objectives, and organization
- developing scenarios
- developing MSELs, taskers, and operational activities
- devise an exercise budget and support plan
- devise performance metrics (target capabilities)
- identify exercise site and configuration
- ensure exercise validates preparedness/demonstrates readiness
- select, train, coordinate controllers, observers, evaluators

We already know that emergency plans exist simply to motivate the
imagination and tax our creativity in assessing the actual risks, hazards, and
expected disasters we know are part of our natural environment. We also
know that planning is the exquisite process of defining risk situations, devising guidance for emergence from those risks, and outlining effective mechanisms and procedures for reducing losses, injuries, and damage in the midst

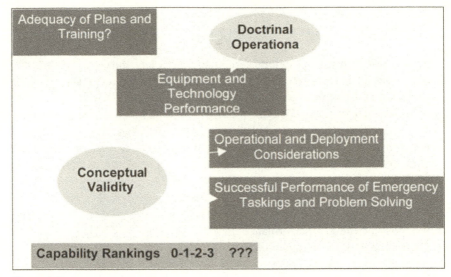

Figure 4.1

of a real crisis. Nevertheless, we also grasp the value of emergency plans as the stage upon which we test our assumptions, beliefs, and strategies for dealing with genuine emergencies—the stage that is brought to life through the development of a sensible and challenging emergency exercise. Some of the boilerplate issues that we expect emergency plans to contain are:

- Comprehensively capture facilities and target risk
- Identify crucial infrastructures and their risks
- Designate special risk zones (tag and track)
- Isolate best prevention-mitigation measures
- Examine related risk-reduction measures
- Outline emergency procedures, policies, protocols
- Provide detailed operational guidance
- Specify evacuation-relocation and shelter-in-place instructions
- Pinpoint emergency assistance resources
- Provide basis for training safety, security, and senior staff
- Provide basis for an exercise plan and annual drills
- Enable site assessment with targeted vulnerability evaluation
- Risk assessment (identify system vulnerabilities) and risk zones
- Address safety and security issues
- Address communications, telephone-and-cyber message issues
- Identify especially high-risk zones (map sensitive areas) hazmat
- Train support and coordination staff on crisis response
- Outline specific scenario-based crisis steps for key personnel

- Summarize emergency procedures for civilians
- Establish and test external emergency notification steps

It is a staggering assumption often made by many that simply outlining these issues in a comprehensive plan means that they are presumed to be understood and that emergency responders have no need to train or exercise to validate their readiness. We know too well that this is a dangerous and ill-conceived set of assumptions and so we are reminded that *emergency plans are meant to be exercised and subsequently improved as a result of exercise outcomes and lessons learned.* We cannot lose sight of the overall focus of exercises when they are designed to simply validate emergency plans. Here are the main reasons why exercising the emergency plan makes sense:

- Establish or validate performance metrics
- Determine equipment capabilities
- Apply technologies to distinct scenarios
- Verify performance of well-known tasks
- Verify performance of novel, unique, or unexpected tasks
- Validate relevance of training
- Validate clarity of policies, protocols, and procedures
- Confirm risk-based readiness (all-hazard variables)
- Observe, measure, stress problem-solving skills
- Determine leadership dynamics
- Track coordination and communication

Turning to the task of exercise focus, objectives, and organization it is understood that they comprise an interrelated package of concepts that must be harmonized in order to ensure a coherent and effective exercise. Exercise focus relates to the broad risk-based or scenario-based situation you want to exercise: hurricane preparedness, hazmat response, radiological emergency response, tornado risk reduction, and whatever else could be framed in a short phrase. This is your overall focus and this is the main theme of the exercise. Exercise objectives have been reviewed and summarized in previous chapters, but the main idea is to *isolate and specify the handful of important performance objectives you want to test and validate during the exercise.* Is it firefighting at a warehouse with toxic chemicals? Is it marshaling employees, citizens and tourists away from a hazmat risk site? Is it informing the local area of impending tornado risks and providing guidance for their shelter? We know that several objectives may be pursued in an exercise, whether it is a TTX or a full-blown deployed exercise. The key idea is to enumerate and specify what those objectives are and prepare to devise activities and taskers that will enable first responders to demonstrate they can handle the assignment. Finally, the organization of the exercise will be largely driven by the initial excursion into focus and objectives. It will become clear whether a TTX will be satisfactory to the citizens, political leaders, first responders, and the media, who share a common curiosity about whether the first responders are as ready as imagined.

In our careers and lifetimes we have witnessed exercises that were accomplished purely for political satisfaction, or to demonstrate that people and gear could be mobilized, without regard to the emergency task at hand. The intent of the "fluff" exercises was simply to show off the equipment and display a dramatic masquerade of emergency readiness when, in fact, no stress, demands, or difficult problems were ever levied on the responders. This is a situation we want to avoid at all costs, as it diminishes our sense of readiness, insults first responders, and betrays taxpayers and citizens alike. Before going ahead with a discussion of other relevant issues central to exercise organization and structure it is useful to review again what the main thrust of exercise design is about. Ensuring that we understand what the main ingredients are for effective exercise design, the ideas are offered to allow a diversity of approaches that best suit the city or village, university campus or hospital, business district or manufacturing plant that wants to take these ideas and adapt them for use to the benefit of workers, citizens, and first responders.

If you have a plan for continuity of operations (COOP plan) but you have never exercised it—you should. Communities that assume their alternate site

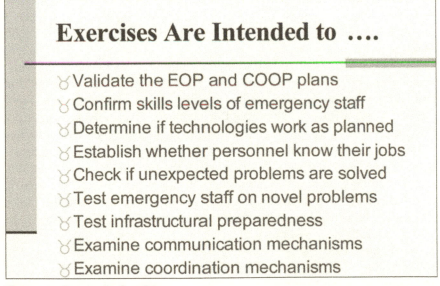

Figure 4.2   Reasons for Exercises.

Elements of Exercise Design

ు Survey of target organization and domain

ు Identify NIMS, NFPA, other requirements

ు Specify performance metrics

ు Develop scenario and schedule

ు Outline EXPLAN objectives by function

ు Determine what type of exercise is best

ు Draft MSEL

ు Draft events and implementers

ు Design and specify evaluation metrics [EEG]

ు Rely on expert team to draft EXPLAN

Figure 4.3   Elements of Exercise Design.

is OK without testing the realities of hasty evacuation and realignment are kidding themselves. Mysteries will continue about COOP until or unless it is actually tested and the hidden issues are revealed for all to see. Testing Continuity of Operations Plan (COOP) assumptions, procedures and strategies is as essential and dynamic as having the COOP plan itself, and it offers a dynamic essential and endemic to COOP itself, and it offers a unique opportunity for local community colleges to partner with their towns and create mock EOCs for student training that could be wired and equipped to become actual COOP EOCs in a real emergency.

The media will sometimes know when things are being done in a professional manner but they can be fooled. Their perception of what happened and how well it was done is crucial to the overall image of first responders—here the media have a powerful influence. But seldom can the media spot all errors and oversights in a complex exercise; instead they target significant activities trying to discern when something's amiss and indicative of a shoddy, substandard, or spurious operation. We owe each other, the media, our community, and our skilled first responders the value of knowing they can do what is required and do it well. Summarized on the following chart are the major elements to be considered and included in any exercise design whether it be a TTX or a fully deployed event lasting three days or more.

Developing scenarios is the next issue to address when examining the organization and structure of exercises. Scenarios do not require an extensive amount of detail but they must be credible, understandable, and demanding.

Photo 4.1   Responders decontaminated after hazmat or chembio threat situation.

They must articulate requirements for emergency performance that not only call on first responders to appear and tackle the crisis but to conclusively demonstrate they can manage the crisis until it is brought under control and safer conditions can be restored. The major factor in exercise scenarios is that they accurately and comprehensively depict the potential emergency situation, including all relevant facts and issues to be considered outlining the principal emergency response activities expected. There should also be enough credible ambiguity in the scenario—just like life—where certain unknowns remain part of the initial scene.

Key Elements in Scenario Development

Scenario development is a key factor in overall exercise design and it must adhere to a few guiding principles in order to reinforce the emergency exercise enterprise. In devising an appropriate scenario for demonstration of emergency response effectiveness certain fundamental variables have to be considered

- What behaviors and tasks reflect minimal levels of effective performance?
- Are there time, personnel, equipment or resource constraints to consider?
- Will key response tasks be completed primarily by community first responders?
- Will outside federal, military, or other resources be necessary?

Here the primary focus in scenario development, aside from depicting the emergency situation and demands as realistically as possible, is ascertaining whether the emergency response set of key tasks can be performed solely by local first responders or whether some form of external augmentation is needed. This could come from federal, military, NGO (non-governmental organization) or other similar sources. The testing of local community first responders in terms of essential relief tasks should be inside the performance envelope of what they are capable of doing—in other words it should not impose unique or unrealistic burdens and demands on that staff which would exceed normal expectations.

For example, complex CBRNE (Chemical, Biological, Radiological, Nuclear, and high Explosive) scenarios ordinarily would be far beyond the capabilities and resources available to most local community first responders. Instead response staff would likely be augmented by special military or federal agency personnel with appropriate technology and specialized training. However, some smaller and more manageable hazmat scenarios may well be within the capacity of local community first responders making exercise scenarios which deal with that situation much for fair and realistic in terms of assessing effectiveness.

Here are a few challenging emergency situations listed below which ordinarily would be beyond the capacity of most local community first responders, however they would open the door to collaborative and joint exercises with appropriate state, federal, and military augmentation personnel. They are, for example:

- Extended (multi-week) collapse of the energy grid
- Mass casualty events with injuries exceeding local hospital capacity
- EPZ (evacuation planning zone) exercises proximate to nuclear plants
- Catastrophic quake/flood/tsunami/hurricane
- Terrorist attack on a school or college
- Sweeping pandemic with uncontrollable spread of disease

In such situations, the development of the exercise scenario must address the likely mix of personnel, special equipment, resources, and risks of unified command structures which can often take the onus of ground zero emergency management away from local community first responders. Here the basic task of scenario development rests on the scope and scale of the exercise itself—how many response organizations are involved? What special personnel and technologies may be required? How long is it expected to take for the disaster zone to be declared safe and free from further residual risk? And how extensive and complicated is the cleanup and remediation agenda following resolution of the disaster itself?

Real resources, real limits, real constraints, and real impediments must be factored in to make the scenario realistic and the scenario should be in the range of possible to probable. That means the likelihood of this scenario happening is within the range of 25–65 percent certainty with ample allowances for unexpected, challenging, and difficult crisis problems to address from the onset of the crisis until its conclusion.

The development of MSELs, taskers, and operational activities that form the actual nucleus of the exercise can originate with a variety of sources. Ideas and experiences gleaned from fellow emergency managers, ideas and insights gathered from after-action reports, concepts and issues derived from LLIS—the FEMA-based Lessons Learned Information System—and many other places are the grist needed to engineer a challenging and useful exercise. Take nothing for granted and assume that a certain level of expertise and performance quality is expected of urban first responders whether they are in Denver, Dallas, Davenport, or Darien. The common denominator is the ability to explain the problem or task at hand, specify the operational requirement to be satisfied, and allow first responders to demonstrate their capability to do so within the confines of the artificial exercise environment. Magic formulations of MSELs or exercise taskers need not be complicated or overly technical, but they must be clear and understandable.

The arrangement of data on an MSEL is to specify each event, the timing of the event's introduction into the exercise, a summary description of the event (this is really better known as a tasker), and then specify the first responder who should get the tasker, the expected outcome, and finally any special

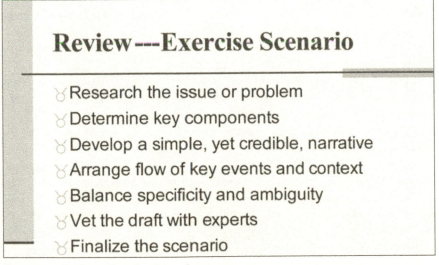

Review—Exercise Scenario

ﹾ Research the issue or problem

ﹾ Determine key components

ﹾ Develop a simple, yet credible, narrative

ﹾ Arrange flow of key events and context

ﹾ Balance specificity and ambiguity

ﹾ Vet the draft with experts

ﹾ Finalize the scenario

Figure 4.4   Review—Exercise Scenario.

Figure 4.5   Review——MSEL Structure.

controller guidance that may be necessary related to the tasker. Table 4.1 illustrates these separate features and displays how they would be arranged on a typical MSEL sheet.

The tendency among most practicing emergency managers is to use some basic variation on this theme as a basis for exercise design. Notice that each event has a number and they are arranged in a time-phased sequence that the exercise controllers oversee. When a particular event or tasker is identified, such as *EOC activation* or *hospital ER reports patient numbers*, these items are summarized typically in one sentence on the MSEL followed by a designated recipient of the tasker and a separate column that *summarizes the expected action or a listing that depicts the range of expected actions that the assigned recipient must execute or perform.*

As part of exercise design, an elaborate and very detailed description of the tasker is given to the recipient and evaluators or controllers will be noting the actual time of receipt as well as what the tasked person decides to do with the new event. It is important for exercise flow and overall continuity management that exercise designers and controllers become aware of the various additional follow-up messages and injects that will be issued periodically during the exercise as a follow-up to each initial tasker.

EMACs (Emergency Management Assistance Compacts) between neighboring communities ordinarily are designed to alleviate high impact demands

Table 4.1   Diagram—MSEL Sheet

Event	Time	Description	Recipient	Expected Outcome
1	6:07	STARTEX Activate EOC	Fire Chief	EOC activated and staffed within 30 min of notification
2	6:11	Dispatch fire units hazmat event	Battalion Chief	Staging hazmat response on site within 15 min of notification
3	6:27	Injuries on scene identified—EMS and hospital ER notified	EMS units Hospital ER	Triage and transport injured by category to hospital ER within 15 min of identification
4	6:38	Request EMAC assistance/support	EOC Fire Chief	EMAC assistance sent—Incident Commander advised
5	6:44	Evacuation of surrounding area out to 0.75 miles	Incident Commander (IC)	Evacuation order delivered by EOC and police NLT 7:00
6	6:54	EMAC crews arrive to assist IC	IC coordinates for enhanced IC	EOC notified Law enforcement & Public Works assist on traffic control

on emergency resources that must be regionally shared. If a tasker is issued to request external EMAC hazmat assistance for a complicated chlorine spill on the interstate, exercise evaluators will be examining players to see how they execute that assignment, how they follow through, how they stage and coordinate EMAC assistance, and how coordination between the incident commander and successively arriving support units is arranged.

Evaluators will have a booklet of serialized sheets that depict each event by number so they can track subsequent responses and actions by recipients to examine how they handle the task and whether they invoke new or unique approaches to solving the crisis.

In freeplay or unscripted situations where very little follow-on tasking occurs and the job of recipients is simply to resolve the crisis, the evaluator will be observing how well the responder handled facts, ambiguities, uncertainties, technologies, resources, and problems. This will also be done in carefully scripted exercises but the overall effort to capture and codify what responders do in a freeplay or unscripted situation is vital to understanding the degree to which "cookbook" solutions work versus innovative solutions that produce the same crisis-ending outcomes.

Remember, *the MSEL aims for the best possible response*, in many cases the correct response is unattainable because of differences of opinion among experts about what approach is actually the "correct" answer. Having coherent EOPs with standard operating procedures (SOPs) for most situations is helpful—but often this is not available.

[Review—MSEL Master Scenario Events List]
• MSEL describes a situation or problem
• MSEL is intended to elicit 'correct response'
• MSEL is designed to test preparedness and readiness
• MSEL expected to validate performance
• MSEL can text both individuals and teams
• MSEL depicts all events from STARTEX to ENDEX
At 9:45 a call identifies 3 simultaneous explosions within and adjacent to the city's major petrochemical plant. The plant's safety officer reports 10 minutes later that further explosions might occur and it cannot yet be determined if the explosions are accidental or deliberate attacks. Huge holding tanks containing 13,000 gallons of chlorine, sulfuric acid, and benzene are within 30 yards of initial explosions. Residences housing approximately 9,000 people are within one mile of the facility gate. What needs to be done?

Figure 4.6   Review—MSEL Master Scenario Events List.

The task of developing metrics on the one hand is easy because NFPA standards and research on best practices gives you a normal range of expected performance outcomes and the differential levels of quality and effectiveness one can expect. The most basic metric to consider is a three-point scale that specifies *not ready—minimally ready—completely ready*. The traditional *red, yellow, and green* color-coded system is also fine. Overall issues with metrics involve finding a way to usefully depict the completion of a designated emergency response task at the *ineffective—mediocre—outstanding* levels. Metrics make sense only when applied to specific taskers and operational activities, because they must be observable and repeatable. External evaluators must always be able to distinguish mediocre from outstanding performance regardless of the situation or exercise they are evaluating. *There should be absolute consensus between evaluators, controllers, exercise designers, and the senior emergency manger that a particular response activity failed to meet minimum requirements or fell well below performance expectations.*

If it can be determined what factors or influences may have led to the substandard performance, these things should be explicitly mentioned so that reasonable corrective actions can be taken. Indications that a task or operational activity was performed at a substandard level requires the judgment and assessment of at least two impartial, objective, and disinterested experts. This finding in an exercise is not intended to embarrass, humiliate, or discharge an employee, but must always be used for targeted remedial action in the form of training, new equipment, new procedures, or other suitable interventions. The overall aim is to deliver the highest-quality emergency response—nothing less will ever do.

Efforts to develop metrics should include consideration of latest technologies and performance characteristics for special emergency logistics and PPE.

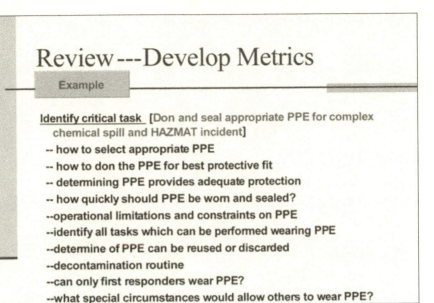

Figure 4.7 Review—Develop Metrics.

In addition, metrics should be applied to the extent feasible in testing the design tolerances, limits, and sustained operational performance of special equipment designed to protect first responders.

One aspect of metrics consideration and scenario development is to test and verify emerging doctrine that places new or ambiguous burdens on cities and communities. An example would be to assess exactly how Defense Support to Civil Authorities (DSCA) would be implemented and enacted when a major city requested defense aid in responding to a bioweapons or radiological attack. How would local and defense elements coordinate and clarify their own operations?

In preparing the exercise, planners, designers, controllers, and senior emergency managers must be cognizant of overall costs. Of course, all exercises involve sunk costs to complete—everyone's time has to be covered as well as consultants, external evaluators, and any other support expenses. Hopefully, the city or village, college campus, or commercial operation has prudently budgeted for this. Annual readiness drills are a minimum to verify and validate readiness. Certainly the *cost of doing no exercises at all* will show up at the most critical and destructive time—when a real crisis happens. It is hard to put a price tag on exercises even if we assume one TTX and one full field-deployed exercise annually. It differs from region to region, and is often dependent on weather, personnel availability, exercise site availability, and

finding skilled evaluators. It is also crucial to analyze the manpower requirements needed for an effective exercise and whether standby backfilling of
positions is warranted.

It can be assumed that TTXs are cheaper and therefore more cost-effective,
but they have as their single biggest drawback the "illusion of confidence"

METRICS DEVELOPMENT

Example

What are critical minimum performance standards for
-- responding to chemical explosions
-- conducting water rescues
-- extracting victims from collapsed buildings
-- coordinating evacuation from a coastal city
-- supervising debris removal after a tornado
-- coordinating mass casualty triage operations
-- determine if PPE are safe to be reused or discarded
-- coordinating decontamination routines

Figure 4.8   Metrics Development.

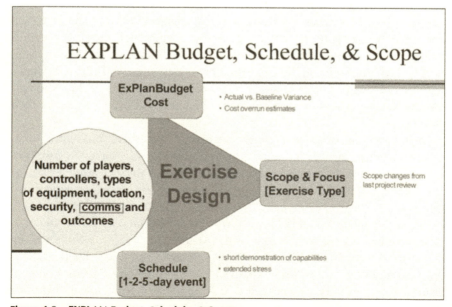

Figure 4.9   EXPLAN Budget, Schedule, & Scope.

problem because tabletop discussions, no matter how candid and detailed, do not replicate actual deployments and do not reflect the peculiar problems and demands one finds in deployed field events. So towns, cities, and college campuses should work together with citizens and the private sector to find cheaper ways of doing full field-deployed exercises because there is no substitute for the experience and insights one derives. However, budgeting for a TTX of one business day will likely cost approximately $30,000 and a full field-deployed exercise may cost four times as much for a full day of eight to ten hours on site. These are not trivial costs, but the alternative is to let everyone stay packed up in the firehouse and hope that when the real calamity comes we are truly prepared and ready.

Another important issue that often gets neglected in the overall scheme of exercise design is the question of whether the EOC itself needs to be tested, verified, and validated. Some smaller EOCs may be filled by communications staff or a dispatch center, while larger urban EOCs are staffed every hour of every day. Therefore, some feel that an EOC running 24/7 for routine operations does not need this extra burden and, in fact, it is superfluous and wasteful to do so because the EOC just increases its "optempo" on demand when a real crisis occurs. These views are understandable, but without an exercise to test the EOC one will never know whether it can function in a smarter, more effective, more efficient, more focused way. This is yet another reason why partnerships with local colleges will help, in the sense that an on-campus

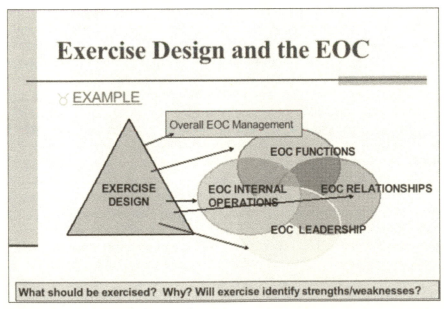

Figure 4.10   Exercise Design and the EOC.

EOC mockup becomes the alternate EOC, it becomes a place to train students on EOC and emergency issues, and finally it allows testing of EOC operations without distracting the real EOC or taking it temporarily offline. EOC functions, relationships, leadership, message management, and other issues can be sharpened this way.

Finally, there are issues germane to the physical layout and configuration of the exercise site itself. Where should it be? What type and level of security should it have? Will the real media have access? Does it make sense to have response cells, controllers, evaluators, and security personnel all jammed under the same roof with communications and IT staff? What about guests and VIPs? Will exercise controllers and evaluators have completely free access to all areas? In smaller jurisdictions, exercises must be one day in duration—how do we maximize the exercise experience for all concerned? Will players be restricted in their movements during the exercise? Where will they be billeted if the exercise goes on for several days? How will logistics, provisioning, supplies, and other logistical matters be handled? Will phones and computers be scrubbed of all exercise-related notes and message traffic? Will response cell staff be able to talk with players? What special provisions are necessary for health, medications, safety, and food arrangements?

Exercise design is all about finding suitable, manageable, low-cost ways for first responders, EOC personnel, and all other critical emergency staff to display and demonstrate readiness. The capability of first responders and emergency personnel to successfully deploy, transit safely and effectively to the crisis site, stage their equipment, establish incident command, determine the most effective response strategy, and execute a professional emergency response cannot be taken for granted. In many cases, communication breakdowns and errors are the single most recurrent culprit in determining whether an exercise "went wrong." This is the very heart and soul of most exercises and it immediately surfaces issues and activities that must be observed and evaluated by trained and experienced personnel who can identify communication dynamics. In addition, examples of expected readiness for each critical task, activity, or emergency operation, when carefully compared with the actual behavior of first responders observed in an exercise, form the initial yardstick of readiness and can be helpful. The key challenge is: readiness compared to what? Is it the NFPA standards, state standards, other standards? Criteria for determining readiness must be clear and unequivocal with accepted neutral standards that form the metrics for evaluating what exercise players actually do. Gaps between ideal and actual performance in such exercises are priceless insights and peerless glimpses into what happened versus what needed to happen. People should not be faulted if their performance doesn't meet the ideal, just as players should not be extolled and lionized when their performance is clearly mediocre.

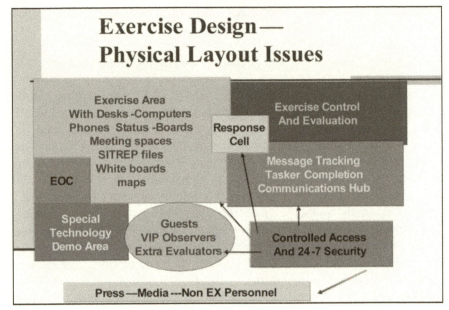

Figure 4.11   Exercise Design—Physical Layout Issues.

What matters most to professional emergency managers is that *the major elements of effective emergency response have been performed at the highest possible level of quality for each enumerated task, activity, or operation.* This does not ask too much of players but creates a standard of expected professional performance to which all personnel in the business eagerly aspire. This is exactly the level of quality and professionalism we really want: We can discern the mediocre, the lackluster and the fanciful from performances that are truly impressive.

Our goal in measuring readiness is to provide a performance standard that all can strive to meet and to motivate improvements in emergency staff and responders that fairly and reasonably persuade higher levels of quality at each successive opportunity.

Measuring Readiness Matters

- Deployment to crisis/disaster scene
- Command linkage with EOC and its connectivity to all players
- EOC management of crisis communications
- Performance of essential emergency tasks
- Timeliness of performance
- Effective uses of equipment/technology

- Coordination-communication issues (interagency and intra-agency)
- Problem-solving (scenario-based)
- Resolution of novel/unexpected events
- Emergency Close-Out/Incident Control/remediation/render-safe

These individual criteria for gauging readiness are fair standards worth exploring, and they will have reasonable target times attached to each specified readiness measure based on the complexity of the emergency scenario; the extent to which proper equipment and logistics are available; and the scope, depth, skill, and number of emergency first responders on hand. Many of these activities and tasks will require significant leadership and coordination skills by incident commanders in conjunction with EOC staff while others will simply compel the natural leaders and innovative people among first responders to step forward and accept the challenge of the situation. *Performing all required emergency response tasks, operations, and activities at a consistently high level of professional quality that enables the eventual management and control of the emergency situation is as much as anyone could ask. This is a fair and reasonable standard for readiness—it must remain so.*

Finally, this chapter intends to summarize all we have thus far discussed by stressing the importance of selecting experienced and skilled personnel to be designers, controllers, coordinators, and evaluators. If the emergency manager is the exercise designer, that is fine; that person also may have the

Exercises Measure Response to Identified Vulnerabilties

- Demonstrates....
  -- response is appropriate [staff/resources]
  -- response resolves problem/ends crisis
  -- response reduces vulnerability

Illustrates whether emergency response sufficiently and conclusively addresses the vulnerability or only provides a temporary solution

Figure 4.12   Exercises Measure Response to Identified Vulnerabilties.

option of hiring outside consultants. In any case, the determination of who will control and coordinate the exercise, as well as the task of finding suitably experienced and trained evaluators, is the toughest of overall exercise planning and orchestration issues. Controllers and coordinators should be very senior, should be external to the area or jurisdiction being exercised, and should have at least ten years of solid emergency management, incident command, and crisis response experience behind them. It is the controllers and coordinators who will ordinarily select and hire the evaluators. Evaluators should be neutral, objective, and removed from the specific area or jurisdiction where the exercise will take place. Evaluators should have at least ten years of operational experience in emergency management, exercise design, and incident command so their own professional experiences enable profound insights into their observations and commentaries. Evaluators must be good writers, good analysts, and be willing to probe into the reasons why certain operations worked and others did not. Most of all, evaluators and exercise controllers/coordinators must work together as a coherent and unified team drawing good ideas and sensible innovations from each other while retaining professional neutrality about the staff and personnel who are exercising.

QUESTIONS

1. What is the role of emergency plans in exercise design?
2. What are the main issues in developing exercise scenarios?
3. What are the main ingredients and features of a MSEL?
4. Why are exercise metrics and readiness standards so important?
5. Why should some exercises include scenarios beyond local capability?

YOU TRY IT—RESEARCH TASKS

1. Develop exercise scenario and MSEL for the first two hours of a crisis involving a major interstate highway bridge collapse within three miles of your town, which occurs immediately following a tornado warning for the county.
2. If the above exercise was designed as a TTX, what metrics would you use to evaluate performance of the EOC and first responders? Why?

Chapter 5

Exercise Control and Management

Without doubt, one of the most important issues which exercise designers must wrestle with as a prelude to the design process itself is a frank and exhaustively specific examination of the actual space, venue, and facilities where the exercise will take place. Key questions of fundamental value must be weighed as the exercise plans and budget are developed. It is not enough to have a ten-acre remote site with trees, fences, and pseudocommunity street layouts and a complex electronic support infrastructure to allow observation of exercises players from any vantage point, although many would be envious of such an arrangement. One basic issue is to determine whether your exercise objectives will be satisfied if the entire event is indoors or outdoors, whether all manner of unpredictable weather and external conditions exist to impinge on players or whether that is explicitly undesirable.

Exercise controllers and evaluators will ordinarily have a significant role to play in designing the exercise and determining the basic scenario, MSEL, and principal taskers. However, it is not uncommon to have contractors or external subject-matter experts (SMEs) hired to perform these tasks. It should never be assumed that designers and controllers will be the same people, although many jurisdictions want this to ensure a degree of purity and consistency in the exercise itself. Greater objectivity and perspective can arguably be secured by bringing in outsiders, SMEs, or a combination if the principal goal is greater objectivity. This is an area of some controversy and finding controllers and evaluators with the requisite skills to do the job and render an in-depth, objective, and useful assessment is the most important consideration by far.

Exercise control must focus on its primary responsibilities and ensure they are enacted with professional and effective detachment. Their primary reason

for being is found in the principle that *controllers are the boss* when it comes
to selecting people for this crucial role. Whether they are called controllers
or coordinators, their role is to determine how the exercise will be enacted
including its overall schedule:

- determine how response cells are staffed
- determine how players will be briefed
- determine what evaluators will focus on
- determine how and when adjustments to exercises are needed
- determine all ground rules for exercises
- determine safety, security, and operational requirements
- determine how the exercise will be concluded including hotwash
- supervise the completion of the AAR
- provide input to any final corrective action program

Hence it is vital that seasoned and experienced emergency managers, or
SMEs, serve as controllers because they will have the skills and experience
necessary to fulfill and discharge this array of responsibilities effectively.
*It is highly recommended that this expertise be chosen from staff outside
the jurisdiction being evaluated.*

While the controller is intimately familiar with the exercise objectives,
MSEL, and detailed taskers for the exercise itself, they must also be adept
at selecting or guiding the selection of observers, response cell staff, support
communications and logistics staff, as well as those external SMEs whose
expertise is deemed essential to make the exercise realistic and effective.
Choosing the right talent is crucial and will make a difference. It is also
important that controllers have mapped out the detailed location and supporting logistics that will undergird the exercise site itself. They must bear ultimate responsibility for security, communications, media relations, logistics,
safety, standby medical support, observers, visitors, and the overall management of each sequenced tasker, inject, or operational activity integral to the
overall exercise.

Physical layout of the exercise site is a significant issue that commands the
full attention of the controller and cannot be delegated to any other exercise
official. This will automatically entail issues of safety and security where
badging, access, identifying authorized persons, and settling questions of
observer/evaluator domains of free-ranging behavior are clarified. The EOC
director and his immediate staff should have a space reserved for them apart
from the larger EOC facility office arrangement itself. Supplies and equipment essential to realistic EOC operations must be included. This means
that copying especially sensitive documents, diagrams, blueprints, and other
materials deemed crucial for player reference and use during the exercise

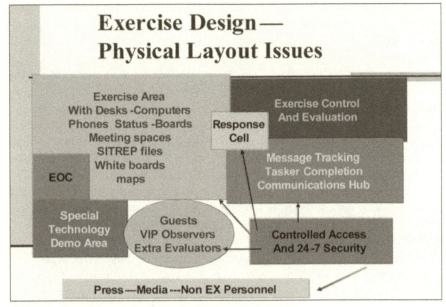

Figure 5.1   Exercise Design—Physical Layout Issues.

usually rests with the controller rather than all players collectively. Determinations, which are normally coded by color on badges will designate who has either restricted or unlimited access to all or selective areas of the exercise site. It stands as a general rule that political officials, approved observers and onlookers, the media, as well as invited guests must be closely monitored and escorted during the exercise at all times. Serious consideration must be given to ensuring that only those persons integral to the exercise will be granted a degree of *articulated access* to all parts of the exercises site. Of course, this will require that genuine external security be observed to preclude interruption and ensure that only properly badged personnel with a specific designation for the exercise access can get inside the actual exercise zone. For example, evaluators, controllers and some SME observers will have the appropriate code (i.e., green—photo—date—unique exercise number), while players will normally wear yellow-coded badges, and response cell personnel ordinarily wear red badges. This means that communications and logistics support staff will also get a separate designation, blue, to denote they are strictly there for support of the exercise. Any and all visitors and other personnel will normally display a badge with *a large V symbol* that is enumerated by a unique number and date to control the type and number of external visitors. Controllers cannot afford to have distractions, interruptions, and unexpected interventions take place while the exercise is being conducted.

In the overall scheme of things badge color is less important that ensuring there is genuine security, accountability, and immediate identification on all badges to allow controllers, evaluators, players, and security officials to know who is who.

It behooves exercise controllers to ensure that several days before the actual exercise begins that a complete review and inventory of the site is completed that would also include a final test of any equipment, systems, or technologies that are integral to the exercise itself. This is especially important if electronic messaging systems, CCTV, document security storage, safety systems, approved rest rooms and player eating areas, and other key sections of the site require verification and testing before the actual exercise. The general watchword to controllers is to police, inspect, and review the entire exercise site at least forty-eight hours prior to the actual exercise, testing that all essential and integral systems are in good operating order.

The next area of responsibility that typically falls on controllers is the unenviable task of reviewing the actual exercise plan and MSEL with exercise designers to ensure that all objectives, key taskers, and essential elements of the exercise are well understood by all parties that share responsibility for a successful exercise event. This should never be left to chance, as there will always be some issue, problem, or unforeseen matter that requires a fix, revision, or adjustment. Careful review of the MSEL is very important, so controllers must invest the time necessary to ensure that all aspects of the MSEL are self-sustaining, clearly understood by all parties, and that critical issues of timing for special taskers and activities are delineated.

If all of these preliminary MSEL issues seem resolved then the controller can turn his or her attention to the actual metrics that will be used to evaluate the exercise and the operational standards that will be used as a yardstick to render decisions on player performance. The simplest methods

---

[Review—Exercise Site]

- Limited access—color coded badges
- Closed circuit TV
- Communications tracking system
- Minimal creature comforts
- Security—containment—control
- Meeting rooms and privacy
- What happens here stays here

Figure 5.2   Review—Exercise Site

are three color-coded ratings that provide ample room for evaluator notes and comments. These are typically *red, yellow, and green* to denote less than satisfactory, satisfactory and excellent. Controllers and evaluators, as well as many players may want something more rigorous, specific, and finely honed, like a five-point scale that denotes a range of performance—*poor–marginal–satisfactory–good–excellent*—and that allows a more detailed and candid assessment by evaluators of player performance. Another three phase scale that some may prefer is the one that denotes differences between *ineffective, satisfactory*, and *very effective*. The main virtue of the three point scale is the degree of flexibility it affords in assigning an overall value to the performance observed. Whatever is being measured in the system of metrics chosen, whether it is meeting the NFPA standard or some other criteria that the state or locality deems a hallmark of success and effectiveness, the goal is consistency of standards that are both fair and yet rigorous.

Controllers must be aware of the metric being used because there is a direct and proportional relationship between the relative simplicity and difficulty of exercise taskers and injects, as well as their realism, in making informed judgments about how well players handled different problems and issues. It is good to remember what the overall objective of exercise evaluation is all about.

Another important part of this process is to clearly label all message traffic, MSELs, and related documentation as *EXERCISE*—which is carefully imprinted in background grayscale tones on every piece of paper related to the actual exercise. Document accountability also requires that key documents have numerical tracking numbers or designators so that all exercise materials can be distributed, filed, and accounted for once the exercise is completed. This is an essential exercise security and document management task that seems full of drudgery but is very important. Watching players tackle and eventually resolve complex emergency problems is just as important as seeing

MSEL Design Issues

Outline scenario, taskers, injects, and related major events.

- Establish an overall schedule for the exercise.
- Indicate when injects/implementers occur.
- Summary of injects clearly specified.
- Free-play determinations indicated.
- Real time versus exercise time noted.
- Directors/controllers have final say on event flow.
- Red team/response cells special instructions.
- Exercise communications/task tracking systems.

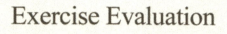

Exercise Evaluation

ᚼ Identify what was done well

ᚼ Identify performance problem areas

ᚼ Identify unexpected problems

ᚼ Capture tasker completion

ᚼ Pinpoint tasker 'orphans'

ᚼ Highlight expert insights

ᚼ Get player views on EXPLAN value

Figure 5.3   Exercise Evaluation.

players handle much simpler tasks. Controllers must ensure that players were given a fair and realistic opportunity to demonstrate a capability and they will heavily rely on the perspectives and observations of SMEs and trained evaluators. It is crucial that players get a fair and reasonable opportunity to demonstrate a capability that is essential for effective emergency response and that in situations where technologies are employed the performance of emergency players, and their equipment, can be equally assessed.

Controllers must also take time to instruct, guide, and coordinate how their response cells will perform during the exercise. It is not always clear whether response cells will be always restricted to MSEL taskings or will be authorized to make ad hoc injects that take players more deeply into new, complex, or unexpected issues. This is an important controller issue because it directly affects the pace and complexity of the exercise itself. Controllers must stay on top of response cell activities and be kept abreast hourly of issues or problems that the response cell identifies. One clear distinction involving response cells is to distinguish cells where scripted MSEL activities are authorized and some degree of freeplay injects are desired.

However, *Red Cell* play typically is unscripted and often consists of red cell members testing or challenging a specific player with a unique problem, or taxing a response capability beyond its design limits. Red Cells have been used with great success down through the years in military war games where Red cells were populated with *experts in the doctrine, strategy,* and *tactics of the enemy.* Here is it vital to note that *Red Cells* in emergency exercises are experts in complex and difficult disaster situations with the

[Response Cells]

- Replicate genuine responses
- Act as upper—lower—lateral experts
- Generate their own taskers*
- Track message handling—completion
- Can embellish or modify parts of scenario*
- Help evaluators determine whether the actions taken by the players are satisfactory or not

* done in coordination with Exercise Controllers

Figure 5.4   Response cells

creative energy and resourcefulness to deliberately challenge players in providing tasks, problems, or novel issues that will stress players to the limit. *Red Cells* can add enormously ambiguous and difficult additional issues into an existing MSEL tasker to befuddle, confuse, anger, or distract the exercise players. This may be encouraged by exercise controllers, but caution is required to determine the extent to which the Red Cell taskers and requirements add significant exercise time, persuade players to pursue a tangential issue, or distract players from the primary exercise goals. The idea to keep in mind about Red Cell play is that its explicit purpose is typically two-fold:

1. Directly challenge players with the toughest level of emergency response requirements possible, engaging players in enacting a *complete solution to the crisis*.
2. Force players to reckon with highly complex, difficult, unexpected, and novel issues that reflect the *cutting-edge of known best practices and technologies* with the overall aim of producing the highest-quality of emergency response possible.

This is far more demanding than what is levied on ordinary response cells, whose major responsibility is simply to ensure that players get clear and unambiguous guidance on the taskers and injects that form the backbone of the game and that players essentially respond to each itemized MSEL event and coordinate, as necessary, with other levels of emergency command. *Red Cells are there to stress players to the limit.*

Controllers who have carefully reviewed the EXPLAN, the MSEL, the physical layout, and systems' structural underpinnings of an exercise have done well to establish the basic ingredients of a successful exercise. Setting ground rules for exercise events, confirming security and safety systems work as intended, and verifying that all message transmission, tracking, and receipt issues can be confidently handled is the next order of business. It is also significant that hotwash, AAR, and corrective action improvement plans become reality and that every effort is made to engage all observers, evaluators, and players in the task of gathering insights, perspectives, opinions, and concerns raised during the exercise.

Starting the exercise (STARTEX) and determining how and when the exercise is concluded (ENDEX) is a controller responsibility along with determinations of whether any part of the exercise should be suspended or stopped to redirect players' attention to a key operational issue, or for safety concerns, so that maximum value is obtained. It is wise to designate a security/safety officer whose job it is to ensure all exercise systems are safe; that equipment operates safely; and that all badging, access, Xeroxing, and document-handling matters are under control. This cannot be taken for granted nor ignored.

Testing message transmission, tracking, and receipt are vital exercise functions which, again, are often a controller responsibility but may require the appointment of a supervisory official. Make sure that attention is paid to the use of player event logs, status boards, and maps to determine whether these useful tools actually made a difference for players in understanding the evolution of multiple exercise events.

Often overlooked, this is a requirement that must be managed with fine attention to detail, and often an exercise controller cannot handle this requirement without a trusted and skilled deputy. Compilation of actual exercise traffic requirements and the eventual reconciliation of those taskers with what players actually did is grist for evaluators and senior emergency officials seeking a glimpse into the dynamics of an exercise and to verify performance. Message traffic and its handling is probably the single most important objective indicator available, shedding light on performance, operational problems, and unexpected issues. The record of what happened is meant to be an objective yardstick of player performance and cannot be manipulated, edited, revised or shaded in any way if one wants to find the truth about emergency performance.

Finally, those responsible for orchestrating, designing, and coordinating the exercise will be remiss if they do not pay attention to *creature comforts* ensuring that players and all exercise staff have access to food, restrooms, rest areas, and comfortable work stations. Of course, if the exercise aims to test player performance in awkward, dangerous, or austere conditions to replicate reality, then appropriate adjustments should be made. The overall operational environment where the exercise happens—windy, rainy, damp, muddy, cramped, poorly illuminated, substandard or dilapidated—makes a difference in player performance. Establishing and sustaining the right exercise environment is clearly within the controller's realm of responsibility. If the environment, the facility, the setting, or local conditions are disruptive and distracting, this is not helpful at all and should be avoided as much as possible.

EVALUATOR ISSUES

Evaluators must be cognizant of their primary responsibilities and devote maximum attention to ensuring they have captured the essential issues and itemized those emergency response actions of greatest significance so that a judgment can be objectively rendered on player performance. Summarized below are the major tasks that evaluators should *be prepared to perform with little or no training.*

Evaluators will work with exercise designers and controllers to ensure there is agreement on best ways to plan and organize the MSEL, which ordinarily means these three important groups will have reached consensus on whether the exercise should be a tabletop or a fully deployed field exercise. While host jurisdictions will ordinarily make these determinations based on political and financial considerations, the actual exercise outcomes and likelihood of success will often hinge on whether the experts assembled to coordinate and manage the exercise can agree on the best way forward. Data collection methods can vary greatly and evaluators must be mindful of the relative advantages and disadvantages of passive observation, checklists,

---

[Exercise Evaluation: Key Tasks]

- Plan/organize MSEL- based schedule
- Determine best data collections methods
- Identify criteria to analyze task performance
- Examine problem solving/leadership issues
- Identify key issues/improvement opportunities
- Gather comparative perspectives
- Coordinate the exercise hotwash
- Develop and write the AAR
- Draft improvement plan

Figure 5.5   Exercise Evaluation: Key Tasks

interviews, document reviews, SME consultations, and chronologies of message traffic. In addition, once these data collection methods are established and agreed upon, there is the issue of fixing fair criteria for evaluating actual player performance and enabling a genuine distinction to be made (supportable and unambiguous) between average, poor and superior performance. For example, each approach has its strengths and weaknesses.

Evaluators must be keen to sort out leadership and managerial issues from those matters that reflect a routine or combined group response where procedures are well known and about which there is little disagreement. They must distinguish between group and individual performance issues, whether coordinated consultations would have made a significant difference in the actual response behavior observed, and examine where specific acts of bold initiative made response quality or effectiveness improve. One difficult issue among all emergency responders is the question of what constitutes *the gold standard* of performance on any assigned task or group activity. This is one reason why codification of best practices is so important so that gradations in performance can be calibrated and standards can be fairly established to identify a level of performance that is significantly impressive as opposed to those that are average.

Gathering comparative perspectives from players, controllers, SMEs and expert observers is also instrumental to rendering a fair and objective evaluation because of the likely risks that some will see similar issues differently or may ascertain that certain outcomes were avoidable or not. External emergency management experts may also be useful here in making sure the standards and requirements being applied to players are realistic and fair. To the extent these differing viewpoints can be gathered during the actual exercise while facts and issues are fresh in the minds of players and observers this is a distinct advantage. However, evaluators should recall that gathering this data within fifteen days of the exercise is still valid and forms much of the corroborating material needed to finish the AAR. Some players and observers may not be so open to sharing their views when more than two weeks have passed and the overall reliability of their observations may be tainted or diluted by memory or the tendency to forget key sequential issues as time has elapsed.

The hotwash represents the best opportunity to gather immediate impressions from players and observers and SMEs about what really happened in the exercise and whether controllers felt that players had met the exercise objectives exhibiting a level of performance that was superior or well above average. Hotwashes are normally run by evaluators and they normally entail about forty-five minutes of unstructured discussion where controllers speak first about exercise objectives and whether they were fulfilled, and thereafter is an open and transparent discussion of issues and problems by players and SME observers. Evaluators conclude the hotwash by providing each

Evaluation Methodologies

Passive Observation
Observe players, note performance, capture specific instances of superior, average, and poor player performance/unscripted play results, novel situations, serious problems.

Checklists
Using preapproved criteria examine player performance against weighted scales or indexed standards to distinguish poor from superior player performance.

Interviews
Interview randomly selected players at different levels to determine their perspectives on the overall exercise, taskers, MSEL, and realism.

Document Reviews
Examine MSEL, taskers, message traffic, or player SITREPS and logs to determine how each tasker or problem was handled, looking for any indications of group decisions, internal debates, or evidence of strategies developed by players.

SMEs (Subject Matter Experts—EM, Fire Chief, Police Chief, etc.)
Interview SMEs to assess their views on the extent to which players were handling the crisis, how organized they seemed to be, leadership issues, special problems, or unique player actions that SMEs noted as significant.

Traffic Analysis
Assess message traffic for signs that certain messages were handled efficiently or ignored, whether some were misunderstood or may have been misinterpreted or misread, and the overall timeliness of player reaction and response.

player, SME, response cell staff, communications support staff, all safety and security personnel, and any other key exercise personnel with a very brief questionnaire that aims to extract any overall impressions about player performance, exercise management, or other germane issues where evaluators may want to gain perspective and confidence about the array of views collected. Information gathered from interviews, passive observation, reviews of message traffic, hotwash comments, and SME observations are then all combined into the core components of the AAR.

Normally AARs are expected within twenty-one days after ENDEX and are presented to the senior officials and players who participated in the exercise with the aim of gathering further reaction, recollections, and viewpoints from all involved in the exercise. The final product is *the Corrective Action Plan* or *Emergency Improvement Plan.* This document is delivered to senior political officials and senior emergency managers with a detailed summary of exercise observations, commentary and recommended areas for improvement or corrective action. The CAP or EIP is accomplished within thirty days after ENDEX, and its authors must be willing to stand behind their analysis and explain the basis for their findings and recommendations to elected and career officials who would normally be interested in the final assessment. Remember that this document could eventually be released to the public or the media, and its contents should include carefully crafted language that highlights accomplishments and notes shortfalls without pointing fingers or laying blame. If it is to be taken seriously as near-term guidance to trigger revisions and adaptations to the EOP, its authors must remain aware of its significance and not turn it into a "report card" if possible.

QUESTIONS

1. What is the controller's chief responsibility?
2. What issues should be of paramount importance to controllers? Why?
3. Which exercise seems more difficult for controllers?—scripted or unscripted? Why?
4. What must evaluators focus on to be effective?
5. What objective data collection methods seem best? Why?

YOU TRY IT—RESEARCH TASKS

1. If you were a controller for a major urban county readiness exercise, what factors and criteria would govern your selection of evaluators and response cell staff?
2. In a complex hurricane evacuation scenario involving a coastal town of 75,000 residents and 30,000 tourists, what objective data collection tools would seem best for an intensive evaluation?

Chapter 6

Exercise Evaluation Principles

The evaluation of emergency exercises is a challenging blend of objectivity, subjective judgment, factual interpretation, event analysis, and consideration of expert and player perspectives reconciled to reflect an accurate and complete record of what actually happened in the exercise. This is the principal reason why experts and skilled observers will make the best evaluators because they know the difference between superior and substandard performance and, more importantly, they are willing to share their views and opinions openly without regard to political, economic or personal factors. Of course, some may differ with evaluators observations, either in principle or in terms of the yardstick applied, but the overall integrity of people performing this vital function, and their innate professionalism, can never become an issue. Evaluators are expected to render complete and supportable analyses of what they observe and record without regard to the station, rank, or official position of the group or persons being evaluated. This is expected because the overall aim of evaluation is to frankly and objectively capture all performance by players and categorize it in terms of relative quality ranging from substandard, to average to superior. This is understood to be the evaluator's primary burden—to be both frank and objective.

Without the various insights and observations rendered by evaluators, we could never determine what was working and what was not. We could never distinguish between an acceptable level of performance and a superior one. We could never determine the extent to which training, skills, equipment, and leadership each contributed to the actual completion of an emergency task or enabled responders to find a solution.

Evaluators today have some experience and insights from former evaluators to draw on; however, the overall landscape for evaluators remains fairly straightforward and direct. The first principle is to *call it as you see it.*

Evaluation Principles

- Call it as you see it
- Focus on actual vs expected behavior
- Assess all integral technologies
- Look for leadership/initiative dynamics
- Check for collaboration/cooperation
- Determine if task completion was genuine, effective and complete

Figure 6.1   Evaluation principles.

This means being brutally frank and comprehensive when assessing the performance of players as a team, with the aim of identifying what was done well and highlighting what seemed to be below par. *The goal is to pinpoint areas for improvement, not assess blame.* In this endeavor we do not play "gotcha" to tag individuals, but instead we offer frank and candid observations that will enable people to sharpen their already strong skills and work on those that need remedial effort. Here, evaluators must not take a wayward path toward those who counsel providing only "good news" rather than complete reporting. With human beings there is always the risk of personal bias, but erring on the side of scrupulous objectivity is the main idea. Anything less undermines the exercise and fails to help players.

Another important issue is to focus on *actual versus expected behavior*, where capturing what really happened, rather than what you imagined you saw or writing down an observation that is generous but not accurate, matters most. Here is a short checklist to ponder in contemplating the array of evaluator principles that remain important and that sustain the integrity of the "objective observer" process.

Checklist of Evaluator Behaviors

- Focus on results and process
- Fulfillment of exercise objectives
- What do performance criteria require for each tasker/inject?

- Were performance objectives met? Explain why. If exceeded, explain why.
- What impact did communications have?
- Were taskers understood? Prioritized?
- Were there equipment/technology issues? What worked and what didn't?
- Player coordination/collaboration? Team dynamics helpful? Or not?
- Significant leadership/management issues that affected players?
- Did players and responders seem to have a COP? If not, why not?
- Did all players from most to least skilled know what to do?
- How did players actually find answers and solutions?
- Did players exhibit problem-solving skills? Why or why not?

Evaluators must be mindful of the role that enabling technologies played in the exercise and draw attention to the operation and performance of those technologies. They must also inquire whether technologies were used properly during the exercise, whether they worked as planned, and whether players maximized their use as a resource. One key facet is to look at technology processes and steps instituted to allow their proper use. These observations and insights are key to understanding how events in the exercise unfolded and the degree to which technologies enhanced or inhibited results.

Then there is the role that managerial skills and leadership play in the exercise. One cannot overlook how teams performed and whether they understood the instructions, guidance, or advice that managers and leaders offered. It is especially important for evaluators to pinpoint when leaders and managers did not offer advice, and exercise circumstances appeared to require that such advice was crucial. Here the major issue is whether intervention by leadership would have reshaped or altered the outcome to such a degree that performance of the exercise taskers was either a failure or a success. Evaluators must be keen to observe and note these instances.

During the exercise there are many situations where individual players and team members must either collaborate or cooperate in order to successfully handle a task or resolve an exercise problem. The extent to which this happens, or does not, is also a crucial determinant of what behaviors account for successful or unsuccessful player performance. Players who act alone and develop a masterful solution to a problem may be credited with achievement, or their "Lone Ranger" conduct could put the team at risk and undermine an otherwise effective response that the group felt was superior to any idea that individual players favored. The requirement to collaborate and cooperate is often crucial to first responder effectiveness and it cannot be understated that the risk also arises that individuals who elect to *go rogue* or *go solo* may do so without the express approval or knowledge of the incident commander. Allowing for instances where sheer heroism and forceful initiative converted failure into success must also be captured by evaluators, lest we overlook the role that such behavior often plays in turning the tide in an actual crisis. Outstanding efforts by individuals must be recognized in such a way that individual initiative and creativity are rewarded—not rogue actions.

Finally, the evaluator should focus on *tasker completion* and examine what factors and influences led to success or failure. In exercises, *orphan taskers are those that get put aside in the frantic pace of ordinary exercises.* These are the taskers and injects that are routinely ignored because they were of lower priority or because they required further thought, resources, information, and assessment. Evaluators must be able to chronicle those taskers completed, and the level of performance observed for each one and then identify those significant taskers that were ignored or forgotten. In this way players can spot those issues that may slip through the cracks in an actual emergency and that, if left unattended, can cause serious negative consequences.

Evaluators should focus their efforts on the issues itemized in figure 6.2 and ensure that evaluation sheets and hotwash comments speak to the majority of these issues because they ordinarily are the ones incident commanders and players care about the most. *In most cases, evaluators will need to supplement their objective observations with interviews, but always remain mindful of the need to keep a low profile and avoid distractions, interruptions, or confusion during the actual exercise.* The most important behavioral caution

Exercise Evaluation Focus

- ☑ Task performance
- ☑ Problem solving
- ☑ Leadership, coordination, communication
- ☑ Timely and effective response
- ☑ Response cell observations [SMEs too]
- ☑ Player observations
- ☑ Outcomes reached and objectives met?

Figure 6.2   Exercise Evaluation Focus.

for evaluators is to keep their notes, clipboards, interview comments, and personal observations private until the hotwash and AAR. To do otherwise completely undermines the scope and integrity of the evaluation process.

If exercise controllers have developed guidance or a handbook for evaluators prior to the exercises, evaluators must adhere to the instructions and requirements that controllers establish. If there is no guidance, evaluators must have a detailed meeting with controllers before the exercise to establish their scope of conduct and delineate the expectations that controllers and evaluators have of each other. Thereafter, evaluators meeting as a separate team can hash out the dynamics and ground rules they want to adopt prior to the exercises and obtain agreement on the criteria that will be used to evaluate player performance. *In the toolkit cited below, it is crucial that evaluators grasp the goals and broadly understand each item and how it will be handled during the exercise in advance.* Without these explicit understandings, the AAR and the Improvement Plan are in jeopardy as each assigned evaluator will abide by his or her own methods and standards.

Listed in figure 6.4 are the areas of evaluator emphasis that deserve special attention in any exercise, with the understanding that some exercises will necessarily focus on one issue, problem, or emergency response function. Specific functions such as resource management, financial management,

Figure 6.3   Evaluator's Toolkit.

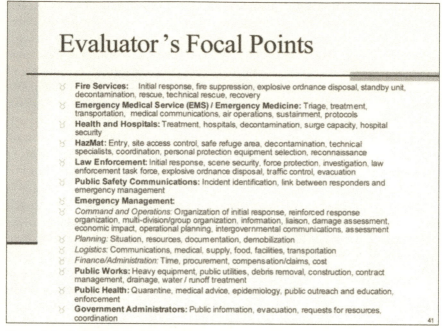

Figure 6.4   Evaluator's Focal Points.

public information, and related activities should be enumerated and targeted by evaluators for attention. Similarly, observing the role of elected and appointed officials, and how they interact, is essential.

Attention to detail matters in evaluation. Independently gauging how different essential emergency functions are actually performed is the very heart of evaluation itself. Rendering independent and objective judgments about the level of performance quality demonstrated is the essence of evaluation activities. Political, personal, improper, and sometimes ill-conceived factors can all be misapplied on an evaluation team to render an assessment that is less than truthful, accurate, and comprehensive. These efforts should be resisted and rejected at every opportunity and unbiased, objective, and firmly rational assessments must be shared with senior leaders, political officials, and the general public unless doing so would create a security breach for the affected community and its staff. The overall imperative is to be transparent and render findings to those having the authority, expertise, and resources to remediate any issues or problems that may impair emergency responders from performing at the highest possible levels.

Figure 6.5 is an example of one evaluator's assessment of how an exercise issue for a particular jurisdiction was handled. The evaluator looked at rumor control issues as they arose during the exercise. Notice the commentary is

Evaluator's Issue Analysis

  Issue: Rumor Control was not provided with adequate reference materials.

  Summary: Several callers were told to contact their local EMA or stay tuned to the local EAS station. However, Rumor Control did not have the telephone numbers for some of the agencies and the radio frequencies for the EAS stations.

  Consequence: Callers were frustrated and felt that they were getting the "runaround" because they could not get the information they needed from one source.

  Analysis: The JIC, where the Rumor Control staff were located, had some of the reference materials and telephone numbers but they were not pulled together in a single resource that could be accessed by all staff. Various staff members had developed their own references. Although staff were willing to share reference information, it was not easy to access and was not available at all when the person who developed the information was not present.

  Recommendation: The EMA should develop a list of EAS stations and frequencies as a reference tool for Rumor Control.

Figure 6.5   Evaluator's Issue Analysis.

intended to be helpful and offer suggestions intended to rectify any problems noted. This kind of assessment would normally be found within the pages of the exercise AAR. Here evaluators are trying to identify issues that, when rectified, enhance emergency response quality.

Evaluating first responder and emergency manager decisions and actions involving complex and unexpected situations like extended power outage and grid collapse beyond 10 consecutive days or postradiological attack city cleanup and decontamination work would require special judgement and involvement by experts before rendering an evaluation. Circumstances and emergencies which are beyond existing doctrine and for which there is no prior experience to rely upon will require an evaluation of how decisions were made and the degree of operational effectiveness and creativity displayed by emergency leaders given their resource limitations and constraints.

Determinations will have to be made as the AAR is assembled to summarize and underscore those salient issues deserving of significant attention during the course of the exercise. One can never assume that given an array of nearly twenty different issues that merit special attention that all twenty issues are equally deserving of prominence in the final AAR. Judgments about the relative importance of certain issues will have to be made jointly by *evaluators and exercise controllers to bring the top five issues forward* for immediate attention. Nothing precludes taking the remaining issues and collecting them into a special annex of the AAR that outlines other issues deserving consideration. Evaluators are trained, and should be briefed prior to any exercise so that their primary attention is devoted to finding examples

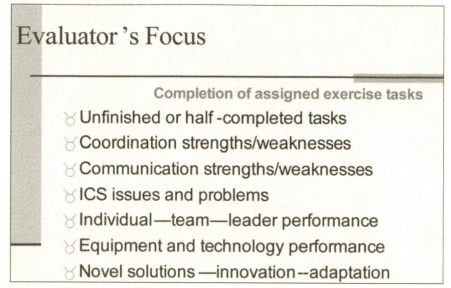

Figure 6.6   Evaluator's Focus.

of high-quality performance as well as instances where performance needs improvement and could be enhanced. It often seems evaluators prepared and experienced for the evaluation assignment are keenly aware of the issues deserving attention. The chart in figure 6.6 highlights those aspects of any exercise where professional evaluators will steer their focus with the aim of expressly emphasizing aspects of emergency response that are fundamental regardless of the crisis being handled.

One issue that deserves special mention is the question of whether the EOP and its guidance proved useful as a resource during the exercise. If it was abandoned or completely ignored, evaluators should inquire from players whether this was deliberate or an oversight. Failure to use the EOP, or rely on it in some instances, may suggest the document is irrelevant or of limited use. This could trigger needed EOP changes. Many evaluators will have a detailed sheet that pertains to each exercise tasker with the intent that completion of the tasker; how well it was performed; and significant issues, problems, and accomplishment are noted. Evaluators will make detailed remarks to describe how a particular exercise event was handled and may interview key response cell officials or others to ensure that his or her initial observations are correct and well founded. As such, evaluator's notes should be considered draft documents and largely unfinished narratives that will be reviewed when the final AAR and Improvement Plan are finalized. In the example cited in figure 6.7, the evaluator notes that relying on the Emergency Management System

(EMS) to keep all relevant parties and players informed may not have worked as intended. Instead the notes outline suggested actions that would either enhance or remediate the identified problem.

Evaluators's Notes [example]

Summary : *(This should be a summary of the events that took place concerning this task.)* JIC staff prepared a series of press releases to convey information to the public. Each release was coordinated with the Executive Management Team. The press releases were distributed over the Emergency Management System (EMS). However, not all counties use the EMS to obtain their information. For example, the Capital County Dispensing Site did not receive any news releases because they do not use EMS.

Consequence : *(This should be a comment of what would happen if the proper actions did not take place as expected.)* Outdated and conflicting information was put out by one county that had not seen the latest press release.

Analysis : *(The following questions should be answered during the analysis: 1. What happened – what the evaluator actually saw. 2. What was supposed to happen – based upon the plans and procedures. 3. Was there a difference and why – conduct a root cause analysis of why. 4. What was the impact – were the consequences of the action (or inaction, or decision) positive, negative, or neutral.)* The JIC relied solely on the EMS as its method of distributing the press releases. The procedures for the JIC require that press releases be faxed to counties that do not have access to or use the EMS. However, when the second press release was sent, the Deputy Public Information Officer (PIO) asked if he should fax the release to the counties and was told by the PIO that it is the county's responsibility to ensure access to and use of the EMS. Capital County has access to the EMS but does not generally use it because staff are not trained for its use. The Capital County PIO indicated that the system was not properly installed and therefore they could not use it.

Recommendation: *(What are the fixes to the root causes? May have more than one.)* The Emergency Management Agency (EMA) should establish procedures or protocols to ensure that news releases reach all affected counties or agencies, regardless of their EMS capabilities.

Figure 6.7   Evaluators's *Notes* (examples).

Evaluation Issues

☒ Safety plan

☒ Media plan

☒ Logistics and administrative plan

☒ Control cell and Response cell

☒ EOC dynamics and metrics

☒ Controller -evaluator-response cell briefings

☒ Player briefings

☒ Ground rules—stop action--suspension

Figure 6.8   Evaluation Issues.

Suggested AAR Structural Outline

I.   Exercise Overview (include one-page executive summary)
    A. Scenario
    B. MSEL
    C. Exercise objective
II. Exercise Activities
    A. Player behavior
    B. Response cell behavior
    C. Major issues and problems
    D. Technology and communications
    E. Taskers and injects
III. Exercise Outcomes
    A. Significant accomplishments
    B. Significant shortfalls
IV. Exercise Management
    A. Controller activities
    B. Response cell activities
    C. Pacing, schedules, ENDEX
    D. Influences on exercise continuity or activity
V.   Summary Assessment
    A. Hotwash comments
    B. Controller and response cell comments
    C. Evaluator comments

Evaluators should also be mindful that all aspects of exercise design, as well as the exercise itself, can be fairly scrutinized with the aim of ensuring the entire experience was realistic, challenging, and useful to all who participated. This is particularly true when evaluating the preliminary steps before an exercise if formally launched. It makes sense to review the safety plan, communications plan, media plan, logistic and administrative plan, instructions for control and response cells, how the EOC is set up and organized to function during the exercise, and whether all players, including evaluators, have been properly briefed about the exercise, its timetable, schedule, and triggering scenario. Reviews of this material cannot be overemphasized because it has such a significant impact on how the exercise is managed and directed.

One issue to keep in mind is the lack of uniform national standards that outline how and under what particular format exercise evaluations should be written. Of course, some states and other jurisdictions will formulate a desired format, but typically there is no ideal "cookie-cutter" standard.

Outlined below is a suggested framework for writing the AAR. The Improvement Plan (IP) is drawn directly from the AAR and cites specific areas needing attention to govern the structure and organization of the IP itself.

Now we have examined briefly the evaluator's principles, focus, and general guidance for embarking on an evaluation. As often as necessary, evaluators should consult with each other and confirm they are keying their attention to the most important issues and using data collection methods that will enable the most comprehensive and transparent report on exercise outcomes and player performance. Delving into specific matters and other dynamics of interest to evaluators is the subject of the next chapter. Here the focal point is grasping what the evaluator's job is and how it fits into the scheme of emergency exercises. No responsibility is as significant or as influential as a professional evaluation.

One final note deserving of special commentary is the broad distinction between emergency exercises intended to test the performance of local first responders and those people at the city, county, township, and suburban level of responsibility who ordinarily are much more worried about natural disasters and hazmat issues than full-blown terrorism, and the officials at the federal level who often get involved only when terrorism is involved or the catastrophe is so widespread—like Hurricane Katrina—that federal multi-state intervention is warranted. Here, one special distinction is the fact that often states are very much in the middle rendering assistance to localities who may be overwhelmed when the disaster surmounts the resource limits of their EMAC or regional cooperative agreement yet find themselves needing police or public safety assistance from the state.

While this textbook deals primarily with local emergency exercises, it can be adapted to address larger and more complex situations where Unified Command configurations may be required. In *Unified Command* scenarios, there is typically a much broader and multifaceted array of players, which makes the exercise inherently more complicated. If this book remains useful as a guide to emergency planners, students, and professionals in identifying the essential elements of exercise design, it will have served its purpose.

The complexities of Unified Command and all the related issues of multilayered command and control schemes is beyond the scope of this book. However, emergency managers should be aware of how the dynamics of multiple agencies and complex coordinating mechanisms typical of Unified Command affect what actually happens. These factors include, for example, some of the following:

- involvement of many federal agencies
- interlocking chains of command at local, state, and federal levels
- external resource and logistic issues where federal agencies are in control

- involvement of military personnel and command networks
- installation of hyper-communication links among federal agencies
- tasking and resourcing decisions generally made by federal officials

In addition, in terrorist scenarios the search for the terrorists themselves, suspicions of secondary attacks and the issue of separating the law enforcement/military component of the exercise from the emergency management, rescue and recovery portion is often difficult to achieve. Large national exercises are often funded annually at a rate of many millions of dollars and exercise planning may take upwards of fifteen months in advance with many dozens of highly paid contractors to set up communications networks, logistics ensembles, and selected SME evaluators. By contrast, most local exercises are starved for funding and must often sustain themselves on a very limited and constrained resource, communications, and logistics menu. Finding experienced controllers, objective evaluators, and skilled communications staff to create an artificial environment, or even to find a suitable location for the exercise itself, in most local jurisdictions is a very tall order. Recognizing these distinctions is important if one wants to be realistic about some of the constraints involved.

This is the central reason why I have long advocated the role of local colleges and community colleges as excellent alternative research facilities, training sites, and areas where useful exercises could be conducted. There is benefit for the colleges and students to be involved in such activity, and there are real cost savings to be derived from staging some major exercise events on campus and using their facilities and resources in a reciprocal manner to build local skills, capabilities, and expertise as well as share insights about best practices. In some cases, campus facilities can be modified to create a mock EOC, which can serve as an actual alternate EOC site for the county, and provide a useful training environment for emergency staff, business leaders, and ordinary citizens.

A prepared and resilient community remains mindful of the influence that limited local resources impose and pushes ahead anyway to be as creative as possible under the circumstances. For example, areas without a local community college or other potential support could seek cooperation with a large company, a major property owner, a warehouse store, or any recipient of government services with the expectation that government is somehow going to take care of them during and following a disaster. They can better understand their role, how they can help the community, and grasp what shared grassroots resilience really means. By so doing, they assume their own responsibilities for protecting themselves and contribute to community readiness.

QUESTIONS

1. What principles should guide exercise evaluators?
2. What is the most important principle? Why?
3. Where should evaluators focus their efforts? Why?
4. What pressures should evaluators resist and avoid? Why?

YOU TRY IT—RESEARCH TASKS

1. In evaluating the public infrastructure and evacuation issues affecting a large waterfront community regularly hit with hurricanes, what issues and factors should form the core of an evaluation?
2. Evaluator interviews of players and response cell staff are crucial. What specific guidelines would you provide to newly hired evaluators responsible for interviewing both groups during a major statewide exercise?

Chapter 7

Exercise Evaluation Issues

There are several issues that evaluators must be cognizant of before they approach the formal arena of exercise evaluation. Each of these issues is significant and cannot be easily dismissed or ignored because they reflect the dynamic forces and pressures that typically accompany the evaluation process. Looking at each of these issues, in turn, we can get a glimpse of their significance and how each one contributes in its own way to the integrity, objectivity, and professionalization of exercise evaluations.

Issues to be given serious consideration because of the important role they play in making evaluations stand alone as objective, transparent assessments of emergency player performance are:

- team training structure and experience
- knowing the scenario and the MSEL
- remaining unobtrusive and neutral
- settling on methodology
- selecting best evaluation criteria
- tracking key events
- keeping an event/tasker log
- developing rapport with controllers and response cell
- being aware of exercise dynamics and environment
- interviewing controllers, response cell staff, and selected players
- running the hotwash
- writing the AAR and Improvement Plan with milestones

We already understand that no two disasters are ever alike, although we can learn from each subsequent event to better prepare for the next one. Nevertheless some common themes should emerge. Many of these factors are self-explanatory and raise no new dynamic issues worthy of consideration. However, we should be honest with ourselves and accept the startling fact that *while all exercises have common structural elements and design principles, no two exercises are exactly alike and each one will likely produce different outcomes and performance results.* This general concept should be widely understood because it helps explain why the same exercise run at two different times, with two different player groups or at two different locations will ordinarily produce nonidentical results. Too many variables, including the random rate and density of player response to MSEL events, as well as the different perspectives players bring to resolving a tasker or handling an inject issue tend to yield differential outcomes. This is not bad—per se—but places enormous responsibility on evaluators to identify and discern what accounts for the differences that may arise.

The most important dynamic that evaluators must track is the "expected outcome" element of an MSEL tasker or inject. Here, the pre-exercise expertise and special skills of planners, advisors, and subject-matter-experts (SMEs) is crucial. If there is a correct and proper way to handle a sarin gas attack inside a subway tunnel, or to respond when a nuclear steam gas release of radioactivity occurs, the set of operational "best practices" rooted in tactical wisdom and experience provide the textbook answer. Of course, when the MSEL outlines a crisis situation about which there is ample controversy and great division of opinion on the "best answer," there are no benchmarks for evaluators to rely on except those that experts have suggested as interpolations of the ideal response.

In addition, evaluators are wise to develop a detailed log that accounts for the major events and taskers that drive the exercise. These logs should accord

---

[Evaluation Dynamics]

- Tracking MSEL taskers/injects
- Task completion [all—some—none?]
- Task analysis—why? Contributing factors?
- Timeline issues
- Coordination issues
- Communication issues
- Leadership issues
- Exercise artificialities? Realism?

Figure 7.1 Evaluation Dynamics.

with the MSEL schedule and briefly focus on the major and most significant actions that players are expected to perform. This effort will be especially rewarded if evaluators maintain a decent relationship with response cell staff and exercise controllers keeping a sharp eye on trends and issues that arise as the exercise unfolds. The task of developing a good rapport with these people enables a fairer and more objective assessment of player behavior and helps provide the foundation for the AAR to be written later.

Evaluation at a professional level requires that observers become keenly aware of exercise dynamics and the overall environment of the exercise itself. Are all players engaged? Are only a few involved routinely tackling issues and problems? Is there evidence that players are relying on their own wisdom and training without recourse to outside technical assistance that may be helpful? Are player managers relying on staff or ramrodding all actions as a function of their authority? Is there evidence of genuine collaboration and coordination among key players?

Sometimes, it is only after interviewing controllers, response cell staff, and selected players that a fair perspective can be gathered on what happened or why a certain event or problem was handled in a particular way. Without a reconciliation of these divergent views, evaluators run the risk of portraying an event through the eyes of only one player thereby distorting the elements of truth often embedded in details that only a merged perspective from all can reveal. In every instance, the evaluator's focus should always be on the completion of assigned taskers, how problems are solved, how managers managed, what communication mechanisms worked or did not, and whether key technology performed as expected. Evaluators should be careful to pinpoint strengths and weaknesses observed to assess whether the behavior players displayed was their own willful conduct or whether their actions were heavily influenced by others or the circumstances evolving during the exercise.

Evaluator's Focus

Completion of assigned tasks
Unfinished or half-completed tasks
Coordination strengths/weaknesses
Communication strengths/weaknesses
ICS issues and problems
Individual—team—leader performance
Equipment and technology performance
Novel solutions—innovation—adaptation

The issue most evaluators recognize as difficult is the staging and coordination of the *hotwash* and making sure that immediate insights and experiences of real significance are captured. Typically, the hotwash runs about an hour and controllers tend to allow players enough time to discuss those issues and exercise events that they felt were effective, logical, and instructive along with those events that were seen as unrealistic, unfair, or unlikely. Some controllers allow evaluators to have about fifteen minutes to review some of the major themes the exercise was intended to highlight and make determinations about whether response cells and players understood the exercise problems in exactly the same way. Here, issues such as tasker value, realism, technical difficulty, complexity, ambiguity, and interpretation can be discussed in an open forum while the exercise is fairly fresh in everyone's mind. In this setting, people can give frank and clear impressions of what they felt was impressive and effective as well as discuss those things that fell far short of expectations. All of these viewpoints are legitimate and must be weighed as one compiles evaluator notes and determines what issues and trends deserve attention later in the formal AAR process.

The hotwash is one of the most important episodes in the entire evaluation because it enables extraction of first impressions, insights, and commentaries while they are fresh in the minds of players, controllers, and response cell staff. Hotwash orchestration requires attention to detail in that the stage-managed event must typically require its completion within ninety minutes and gather as much verbal feedback as possible along with significant written commentaries from all in the room. This means having a prepared questionnaire ready to provide to all in attendance with a boldly printed caveat that this written evaluation is intended to capture first impressions and that within two weeks evaluators will come calling to extract additional information

---

[Exercise Hotwash]

Controllers and Evaluators Lead Discussion

- All players comment and participate
- Gather response cell perspectives
- SME/special observer comments
- Codification of 'top 5 good' issues
- Identification of 5 issues where improvement seems necessary
- Draft summary briefing

Figure 7.2 Exercise Hotwash.

as necessary. The agenda for the hotwash is simple; here is a sample for a ninety-minute session:

- controllers give their overall comments (10 minutes)
- response cells provide their comments (10 minutes)
- players are asked to identify highlights (15 minutes)
- players are asked to identify special issues or problems (15 minutes)
- evaluators remark on major issues (10 minutes)
- general discussion by all about the exercise (10 minutes)
- controllers and evaluators summarize comments (5 minutes) close out
- time allocated for players to answer written questionnaire (15 minutes)

In this way, most of the initial issues including high-value events and problems can be readily identified and a *quicklook briefing* can be given to senior political officials or executives within an hour of the hotwash itself as all players are dismissed and sent home. Quicklook briefings of senior officials do regrettably convey the risk that hotwash impressions gathered may not paint a completely accurate version of what took place. Nevertheless, some jurisdictions will feel pressured and cajoled to offer a quicklook review in lieu of a formal AAR. This should be avoided to stress the value of thorough analysis and detached assessment, which is the heart of a well written AAR. At all times, evaluators should remain as objective and neutral as possible because they are expected to provide a complete picture of all that took place during the exercise. Further, it is important to stress again that hotwash discussions should be frank and without firm attribution. They are not public events nor are they open to the press.

In the final analysis, efforts made to render a complete and professional AAR should be fairly exhaustive, covering every instance of exercise design, structuring of MSELs, taskers, selection of communications staff and equipment, special environmental issues of the exercise site, skills and experience of controllers and evaluators, and the overall schedule and organization of exercise events. Doing so assures a better acceptance and comprehension of the exercise evaluation process and allows readers to get a comprehensive overview of what happened even though they may have never seen the exercise. It is crucial that AARs not be written in a vacuum and that serious consideration be given to examining other AARs before writing the one you are responsible for producing. Moreover, you and the evaluation team writing the AAR should ask yourself a few questions before embarking on the writing process to ensure you have satisfactory answers in mind.

Writing the AAR is not a tedious or complex task but it does require some organizational skills in aligning the themes and issues that evaluators must address in any formal report. It is always good to footnote observations,

[After-Action Reports (AAR)]
• Exercise summary and purpose
• Review of exercise management
• Major areas of accomplishment
• Areas needing improvement
• Suggested remedial actions
• Itemized milestones
• Exercise re-test proposals

Figure 7.3   After-Action Reports (AAR).

where possible, to draw their essence from a follow-up or an on-site interview where there is minimal risk of inserting solely the evaluator's perspective or judgment. Outlining the AAR should be structured to allow as full a discussion as possible on salient issues such as the following, which will also lend coherence and structure to the document.

• Were exercise objectives reached?
• What significant accomplishments in emergency response were demonstrated?
• What issues or problems prevented achievement of desirable outcomes?
• What issues were unexpected or produced novel challenges to players?
• In what ways and what areas did the exercise affirm readiness and preparedness?

These points only suggest the elements of an outline because evaluators must also address the overall management and coordination of the exercise, making mention of the activities and gestures that evaluators and response cell staff used to make the exercise effective. This is also where evaluators can comment on whether players fought the scenario, disagreed with technical requirements, or raised concerns about MSEL events and their realism. Evaluators are often writing the AAR for a limited public audience, the players themselves, and the political leadership of the community that participated. There may be sensitive issues that evaluators and players do not want made public and there may be issues that will stir up political controversy once revealed, but the honor code for evaluators is to be ruthlessly frank, objective, and comprehensive. Of course, there must also be a positive overall tone to the AAR that encourages players to make adjustments or changes that will enhance emergency preparedness and readiness. Most readers of the AAR

[Evaluation Issues]
• Incident command
• EOP value
• Player training or experience
• Clarity of task or problem
• 'One best way'? Or 'Several ways'?
• Genuine demonstration of capability?
• Technology or systems issues?

Figure 7.4   Evaluation Issues.

will be looking for a report that addresses fundamental issues of importance, both to the political leadership of the community and the managers responsible for emergency operations and response. The AAR should address these issues head-on and without any effort to avoid controversy, being careful to remain objective and to support any criticism with interviews, expert observations, or objective assessments from response cell and controller staff.

Another key issue often overlooked in exercise evaluations is whether the players and response cell staff were involved and committed to making the exercise as realistic and stressful as possible. If there are indications that some expected certain taskers, or that some issues raised were considered a joke and some other taskers mocked, that is cause for concern. Evaluators should be especially mindful of those who are not enabling the most complete acceptance of the scenario and taskers, as that will undermine the exercise and undercut its learning value for everyone else.

Being able to back up and justify any criticisms, or recommended corrective actions, strengthens the evaluators position and provides further integrity to the evaluation process. Narrative AAR segments that cannot be footnoted and verified to support an observation may be tacitly rejected by players unless certain key observations can be corroborated and confirmed by another source. This is also why an event/tasker log is so important to identify where some significant event happened during the exercise and to allow SMEs, observers, and response cell people to confirm what evaluators witnessed. Participants and players should be assured at the outset of the exercise that the exercise will levy demands on them to act professionally, as they would in any emergency, and that their individual actions will be observed but are far less important than how the overall emergency response staff handled the problems presented.

In rendering a final AAR, evaluators should be keenly aware of the various extraneous and intervening factors that may affect player behavior and account for a performance that was either impressive or lackluster. They should do this without drawing undue attention to individual errors or oversights, focusing instead on the factors themselves.

Finally, evaluators must come to grips with related issues that impinge on the conduct and management of the overall exercise. Was the site chosen for the exercise good or bad? How did the exercise environment affect player response and receptivity or overall realism? Were taskers and injects clear or ambiguous? Were problems and exercise challenges realistic? Did players discover new insights? There are many related questions worth raising because the emphasis is on finding those external but significant forces that may have affected players and caused different outcomes to occur. It cannot be stressed enough that evaluators are expected to find fault when it is legitimate and uncover instances of brilliant, creative, and effective performance whenever they can. Finding this balance, and being objective and fair in the reporting of it, form the very heart of the evaluation process. Well-designed and funded exercises can still be a flop if the players don't buy in, the taskers are rejected or modified, and emergency performance is marginal but given better recognition than deserved. By the same token, poorly funded and shoestring exercises that are realistic, genuinely test readiness, and effectively demonstrate emergency capabilities, can be roaring successes if they are properly managed and controlled. In that sense, exercise controllers must be assessed as either "masters of the game" or "outstanding directors" and their role in coordinating and orchestrating a successful exercise cannot be diminished. Likewise, in those regrettable examples where controllers did not do their utmost to ensure an effective event, evaluators must be ruthlessly frank and indicate when and how certain controller behavior—not player performance—led to a disappointing result.

[Evaluation Considerations]
• Exercise site conditions/environment
• Clarity of taskers and injects
• Agreement on evaluation criteria
• Players understand roles/responsibilities
• Notification/communication mechanisms
• Message tracking systems
• Capability expectations

Figure 7.5   Evaluation Considerations.

In conducting the hotwash, evaluators must be attuned to player attitudes and views that provide an immediate synopsis of what happened in the exercise. There is always the likelihood that two different players in adjoining functions may have seen a particular exercise tasker differently, or may differ significantly from what a member of response cell staff indicated happened. One of the difficulties that all evaluators must reckon with is the degree to which *divergent perceptions* shape the views of players and some instances will not be readily reconciled if one player claims, for example, that a tasker was ignored while another claims it was partially fulfilled, but the ambiguous portion was deferred. There is no easy way to account for these differences, but evaluators must always recognize they can happen and determine how best to reconcile contrasting viewpoints on a key tasker or event. Here it is significant to note how often comments shared during a well-managed hotwash may seldom emerge afterward in structured interviews or via questionnaire inquiries.

More specifically, it is possible that very direct and candid comments about the exercise will be derived during the hotwash to a degree not normally found in structured interviews, where other factors, intermittent conversation, personal reflection, and similar forces subtly cause people to shift their first impressions and dilute their revelations.

We must consider how the AAR provides the underpinnings of the IP and how the IP itself, as a separate document, becomes a critical product of the exercise and is, in fact, the last official document to be issued from the entire exercise design and evaluation process. The AAR has summarized all exercise activity and captured in a single document, usually less than twenty-one pages, the major activities, outcomes and value of the exercise itself. Only a portion of the AAR deals specifically with certain suggested remedial and corrective actions. In the summary portion, which itemizes the five major

---

[Exercise Controllers]
• Set stage for scenario and exercise
• Launch, coordinate, time MSEL events
• Verify taskers/injects are being handled
• Foster continuous exercise movement
• Manage flow and pace of events
• Determine response cell tempo/focus
• Steer exercise toward intended outcomes

Figure 7.6   Exercise Controllers.

outcomes of the exercise, there is little room for discussing in detail how certain issues or problems will be tackled. Instead, general milestones are often expressed to suggest that for each of the five major issues identified *that corrective actions should be taken before the next exercise where those issues are likely to surface once again.* Soon afterward, decisions should be made about forming a committee of local emergency experts to work on the IP and determine its format, tone, and eventual completion date. Consideration should also be given to briefing elected officials and senior managers.

At this point, the development of the Improvement Plan (IP) is critical because it commits the jurisdiction to certain corrective actions that will either be accomplished within the expected domain of allotted budgetary resources or it will itemize the actions that cannot be implemented without the commitment of additional funds and resources. This makes the IP an inherently political document and one that some jurisdictions would prefer not to pursue. For many, the overall tone and tenor of the AAR is deeply specific about events, capabilities, strengths, problems and recommended corrective actions. Hence, there is no special need for an IP or any other similar document that commits the jurisdiction to find new funding or gather in additional resources. The IP can be of value for those communities seeking onetime supplementary funding from a federal grant where justification for the extra money required is found in the text of the IP. This leaves many communities with an inherent dilemma if the AAR discloses a need, weakness, or problem that should be rectified, there is hardly the political argument and corollary horsepower in an AAR to summon additional resources to fix the problem.

So the best way to summarize the final evaluation issues facing many communities is to become keenly aware of the relationship between available resources and the need to take corrective actions that will somehow enhance emergency response. This can place enormous pressure on towns and localities to "find" superior levels of emergency response when an exercise occurs because nobody wants to highlight a serious shortfall that will require additional funds that are in scarce supply. In turn, this causes one to seriously consider how effective EMACs (Emergency Management Assistance Compacts) really are in compensating for revenue and resource shortages that some exercise AARs indicate are needed to remedy a problem. When cooperating communities work together this is a great achievement and it enhances the level of emergency response. However, it is important to keep in mind that unless an exercise tests the capacity of an EMAC to handle a designated crisis, one continues to rely on faulty assumptions about the EMAC's role and contributing effect to emergency response situations.

Additionally, evaluators should be aware that EOPs often contain specific annexes to address differentiated threats, and it is assumed that the community has the resources, equipment, technology, and training to handle these

[Exercise Hotwash]
Controllers and Evaluators Lead Discussion
<ul><li>All players comment and participate</li><li>Gather response cell perspectives</li><li>SME/special observer comments</li><li>Codification of 'top 5 good' issues</li><li>Identification of 5 issues where improvement seems necessary</li><li>Draft summary briefing</li></ul>

Figure 7.7   Exercise Hotwash.

[Improvement Plans]
<ul><li>Focus on major tasks and activities</li><li>Itemize best practices</li><li>Outline remedial actions</li><li>Determine if EOP needs modification</li><li>Delineate long-term issues [if any]</li><li>Capture and share lessons learned</li></ul>

Figure 7.8   Improvement Plans.

situations without resorting to an EMAC or state assistance. As a reminder, evaluators should check the EOP to see when and how various "special annexes" were ever exercised and whether exercises contained problems and taskers that compelled players to execute these special procedures.

Finally, the evaluator should be attuned to what exercise controllers are doing to manage, coordinate, direct, and sustain the exercise. Look especially at what the controllers feel are the most important elements of the exercise schedule, how they intend to handle unexpected issues, and what steps they plan to take if the exercise veers into a domain of activity that is inimical to the overall purpose of the exercise.

If it appears that nothing is going well, or that certain controller actions are actually undermining the goals and objectives of the exercise, evaluators should be quick to point this out after allowing a certain degree of time to elapse for controllers to realize the error and take their own corrective actions. This is unlikely to happen in a well-designed and professionally managed exercise, but with new staff and those with limited experience there is the risk

[Exercise Controllers]
• Set stage for scenario and exercise • Launch, coordinate, time MSEL events • Verify taskers/injects are being handled • Foster continuous exercise movement • Manage flow and pace of events • Determine response cell tempo/focus • Steer exercise toward intended outcome

Figure 7.9   Exercise Controllers.

[Exercise Evaluations Should]
• Enable capture of best practices • Identify gaps and weaknesses • Pinpoint collaboration/coordination issues • Highlight leadership/teamwork dynamics • Sort out areas for EOP revisions • Draw out areas for improvement

Figure 7.10   Exercise Evaluations Should.

that the exercise will deviate from its intended course. One key job of evaluators is to rapidly recognize when an MSEL event, tasker, or response cell inject has inadvertently launched player behavior into directions and activities deemed useless or nonessential for the exercise. Keeping controllers aware of how certain activities are progressing will enable them to keep exercise activities on schedule and retain an effective and professional atmosphere. This keeps the focus on what evaluations are all about and what evaluations should generally accomplish.

QUESTIONS

1. What are the foremost issues that evaluators are responsible for? Why?
2. What does the hotwash accomplish? How should it be coordinated?
3. If AARs and IPs are distinctly different documents—what distinguishes them from each other?

YOU TRY IT—RESEARCH TASKS

1. If an AAR identifies a major shortfall in necessary technology to enhance emergency response, but that would cost an additional $2 million dollars, should the AAR refer to this issue or emphasize instead a less important issue with no budgetary significance? Why?
2. If a community seeks an IP, should it be assumed that the community is committed to taking whatever corrective actions the IP identifies? Why or why not?

Chapter 8

Exercise Design Considerations

So far, we have identified most issues relevant to fulfilling the basic emergency exercise design and evaluation issues however a few additional considerations deserve to be mentioned and examined in some depth. To a large extent, many exercises which will affect local community first responders may entail eventual collaboration and coordination with external organizations such as state agencies, federal agencies, the military, NGOs and some business enterprises. It would be beneficial to briefly review how these differential factors which are genuinely external to the local community could impact the performance of local emergency responders and actually enhance the overall quality and effectiveness of emergency response operations.

First there is a need to articulate some of the scenarios and emergency response demands and situations where it is most likely to find a significant additional layering of external agencies and organizations owing to the complexity, ambiguity, and challenge which these situations impose. This includes explicit consideration of those emergency scenarios where the helpful assistance normally rendered by CERT teams, for example, may be relatively less important than the kinds of specialized equipment, technology and resources which a military CBRN team can provide. This is not intended to diminish the value of CERT teams but instead emphasize where the degree and scope of risk to the community places greater risk on citizen involvement when hasty or expedient evacuation, shelter or equivalent safeguards make more sense that allowing CERT teams to do what is normally expected of them.

A *second important issue* deals with the nature of the complex disaster, or catastrophic emergency, itself. In other words, the crisis transcends the capacity of local communities to adequately manage the emergency. Here the extent of technical, law enforcement, public health residual capacity and the sheer ambiguity of the scenario itself means that many unanswered

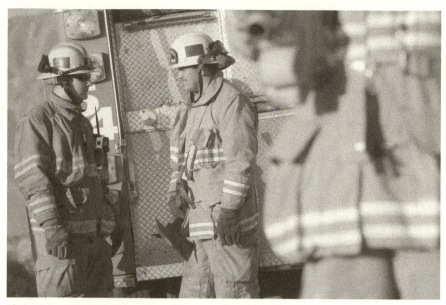

Photo 8.1   CERT (Civil Emergency Response Team) Exercise.

questions attend to the issue of how best to manage the crisis and alleviate further risks to the general public. Some of these situations where complexity, ambiguity and overwhelming technical challenges emerge include these sample illustrative emergency scenarios.

* Widespread pandemic with uncontrollable disease spread
* Nuclear plant explosion and radiological dispersion accident
* Terrorist attack involving CBRNE
* Hasty evacuation of several major cities and towns

Still a *third valuable consideration*, closely related to the second, is the sheer difficulty of prior coordination and operational collaboration with those select external organizations which have adopted and devised their own set of emergency response operations and related doctrine. These organizations, which ordinarily assume that local community first responders will play an integral but largely background role in rendering assistance, will often seek to promote their own operational objectives in ways that relegate local first responders to a supporting status.

In effect, the position being clarified here is that when a disaster becomes inherently federal in nature local communities largely lose control over operational matters. More specifically, federalized emergency operations are basically distinct from normal community emergency response operations because the focus of overall crisis management shifts to a federal agency which is most often referred to as "the lead agency." Some of these situations do not obviate or nullify the value of local community first responders but present the dilemma of shifting overall incident command and coordination to a different level of government. This changes the focus and objectives of emergency exercises where overall incident command and crisis management resides outside the local community. Often this scenario refers to "unified command" situations where multi-state, federal, and military organizations will be directly involved and agencies such as FBI will assume leadership of the crisis in lieu of local emergency managers.

In all three scenario situations described above it still makes eminent sense to actively participate in emergency exercises which convey direct and indirect benefits to local community emergency staff and first responders. Local community first responders can clarify their role, examine the extent of their direct involvement, alert affected citizens of how differently these complex situations will likely be handled and make ready civic advisory groups to expect the variation in external activity and overall direction which federalized emergencies could take.

A final note worth mentioning is the important process of joint and collaborative exercise planning between government and private sector entities. Most disasters will affect both private citizens and industrial or commercial firms to some extent. Prior coordination on relative expectations, assumptions, needs during first the 48 hours after a disaster and onward efforts to recover from it are the essential ingredients of a well-planned community exercise program.

Other Considerations

In addition to what has already been stated, local community first responders and emergency planners must take into account the degree to which local businesses, industrial facilities and related private sector enterprises expect to conduct affairs in emergency situations. The overall thrust of recent Business Continuity Plans (BCP) for large and medium sized business and industrial operations has taken a series of steps toward harmonization of strategies which most businesses recognize. It entails looking at the risk environment, assessing key operations and system failure risks, deciding best possible post emergency outcomes, identifying and prioritizing gaps, devising contingency plans for reduced and resumed operations, looking at critical supply chain issues and relevant power and utility support systems. Their plans for short versus long-tterm disruptions, cyber attacks, natural disaster impacts on

Figure 8.1   Basic Issues of Operational Focus in Ecercise Design.

business operations and other risk areas have become more sophisticated in recent years. The chart below summarizes the kind of BCP issues normally considered by major business and industrial firms.

Having said that, local community planners must reckon with the adverse toll which disasters can impose on smaller businesses who lack the wherewithal to conduct sophisticated BCP efforts. In these instances the value of joint and collective emergency planning and the inclusion of business and industrial elements germane to the local community's well-being makes perfect sense. Assumptions, perspectives and biases which inhabit the plans of local first responders can be shared and discussed with business and industrial leaders so that misconceptions and errors in planning can be smoothed out. Business continuity planning assistance and advise can be one of the most important projects which a community's emergency manager could ever undertake.

This affords an excellent opportunity for proximate colleges to offer selected service learning opportunities to students pursuing degrees in emergency management to engage in observing emergency exercises, participate in risk assessments, become involved in community preparedness training, work with local businesses to reconcile government and private sector emergency plans and contribute to upgrades in revised EOP and BCP efforts. Educational ventures which solidify these experiences can also reinforce academic study of emergency management issues eliciting greater student interest in eventual careers in emergency management.

Another key consideration is working with military emergency planners at nearby bases to discuss and jointly review how emergency plans and exercises can reflect how proximate military bases may be affected. This will also help identify what measures may be taken by base commanders as a contingency when local military and civilian workers who depend on the base for their livelihood must contemplate how normal base operations could be affected by a variety of disasters.

Related to the military set of issues is determining how National Guard and related military augmentation missions could reinforce and enhance local community emergency response operations. Here the focus is on sharing perspectives about a range of threat scenarios, what the Guard is prepared to offer in emergencies, how calling up Guard personnel might affect local communities and examining the array of issues where Guard support and routine Homeland Defense civil support activities might be conducted. This affords an opportunity for joint and collaborative training and exercising which draws attention to the resources, talent and expertise offered by both Guard and local government components.

Questions about extended shelter in place, massive evacuations, temporary relocations and unusual public health emergencies can be tackled in these useful exchanges with both military and private sector planners. The more challenging and ambiguous the emergency the more valuable the insights and perspectives gained from dialog where the diverse interests involved can discuss issues and expected problems openly and frame useful exercises to explore and probe how actual operations may be conducted. Testing the assumptions which all sides bring to the post disaster response and recovery set of actions is critical. These often divergent views about what is urgent and what is not deserve attention.

Another area of fruitful collaboration which can pay real dividends is enlisting the emergency planners from major school districts to discuss their plans for conducting emergency exercises which test not only their own schemes for active shooter and security-related scenarios but exactly how schools may integrate their own disaster planning with local community leaders. The key issue here is comparing risk assumptions and assessing contingencies that ordinarily not overlap between schools and communities.

What factors seem likely to affect both schools and communities in a simultaneous manner? What expectations attach to evacuation, shelter and relocation contingencies when disasters strike midweek affecting schools and residents alike? Are some schools assumed to provide shelter? Are some schools proximate to high risk zones? Exercise designers must take into account how these basic questions are address and clarified in EOP documents. Is there a mistaken or flawed assumption about how emergencies in local schools will affect local public health, utilities or private sector industrial activities?

Exercise planners must always look beyond the obvious and consider whether unlikely scenarios where there is low probability of occurrence but

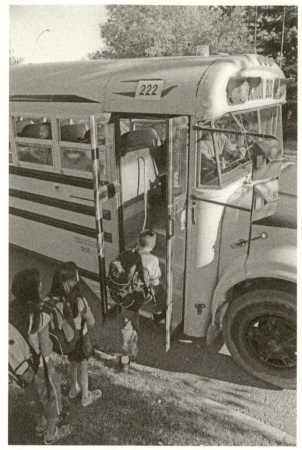

Photo 8.2   School Security and Emergency Response is a Crucial Exercise Issue.

extensively harmful impact. Practicing and exercising for the normal range of expected emergencies is fine however a failure to examine risks and situations that stress and exceed normal expectations should be the norm as well. As the chart listed above explains, it is never enough for schools to prepare solely for the expected "active shooter" scenario and it is risky to assume that the school's EOP has been tested, stressed, and validated against different crisis situations.

In addition, communities proximate to colleges and universities have a special obligation to engage in joint emergency planning with university-based emergency staff to determine what specific risks and assumptions undergird the on campus plans of academic institutions. There may be faulty assumptions about the ability of local communities to augment collegiate emergency staff or there may be technological risks related to chemical, biological or

Exercising School Emergency Readiness
1-school EOP includes different crises
2-school EOP outlines roles for key leaders
3-school EOP tested/validated every 2 years
4-school EOP validated with police/fire Department
5-school EOP discussed with teachers
6-school EOP discussed with parents
7-school EOP covered with students
8-school EOP stress tested for 4 hours
9-school EOP contains media plan

radiological research activities undertaken on campus where local governments have no clue about inherent risks associated with these legitimate university research activities. Attendant to that risk is whether universities retain special response technologies and capabilities to respond effectively in the event of an accident or emergency.

Consideration is also merited as emergency exercise planners examine the historical record of emergency response and the latent observations of prior AAR studies for the community and the region. If the area is prone to recurrent floods, hurricanes, quakes or tornados this should form the foundation for serious exercise planning. Here, the federal and state governments have readily available databases nested in LLIS repositories where systematic reviews of operational lessons learned can be screened and reviewed for applicable value in planning future exercises.

In assessing a variety of exercise options the planner must reckon with the issue of confining and describing the actual parameters of the emergency operational zone. For example, is the exercise zone of response activity a square urban block—or is it a geographic area which encompasses a region or a city and its adjacent suburbs? Is the focus on a solitary building or a grid of closely aligned urban structures? This series of basic questions illustrates the value of devising a risk map which depicts the actual terrain, features, boundaries and key activity areas which form the centerpiece of the exercise itself. Risk Maps can be crude or fairly sophisticated but they should be posted and available to all players and depict key buildings, relevant facilities, roads, bridges, ports, airports, railroads, residential areas, industrial areas, schools, hospitals and main streets as much as possible. This defines the common area of analysis for devising credible solutions which tackle the issues which the emergency presents.

Another key consideration in devising emergency exercises is to examine the array of options which planners can invoke to test and examine emergency response readiness and preparedness for a wide cross section of realistic situations. A number of substantial emergency response and preparedness issues deserve to be tested, examined and exercised as we move forward into the twenty first century. It is foolhearty and dangerous to keep exercising scenarios and issues that are well known and fit well into our comfort zone of predictable disasters. We must repeatedly engage our emergency managers and leaders with challenging situations which reflect the true spectrum of risks and threats we face. That means looking at exercise scenarios which range from the predictable to the very unlikely. Some of these areas of potential focus are novel, others are not, yet they all deserve consideration. This would include the following:

Infrastructure Failures—here the aim would be to zero in on any number of significant infrastructural issues where extended emergencies might occur to include energy sites, transportation, water and public works, and other infrastructural areas where explicit discussion of mixed public and private domains of shared responsibility exist. Infrastructure accidents, disruptions, and failures exceeding ten continuous days should be the central focus here.

ESF Risk Spectrum—focusing exercises on key ESF activities such as transportation, communications, mass casualty care, logistics management, agriculture, energy, and long-term recovery enables community first responders to routinely verify their own level of readiness for emergency scenarios that are realistic, demanding and underscore how EMACs would operate in certain crisis situations. Focus on those ESFs which are routinely expected and allow for periodic exercising of those which are not.

COOP (Continuity of Operations)—the main idea here is to test and examine how COOP plans for the city and its key resource elements would actually perform under stressful COOP scenarios to delve more deeply into stressed communications, public safety, utilities, and related functions. Testing would focus on local, regional and state connectivity, coordination and collaborative emergency response.

Incident Management—the central objective of these activities, which would normally entail a series of tabletops focused on key infrastructures, major areas of private sector industrial activity, areas of persistently high risk and facilities which have always presented special security challenges is to examine how emergency command leadership teams actually function. Emphasis here is on coordination, communication, collaboration and problem solving within the context of scenario-specific situations where recurrent judgments and progressive assessments are expected and essential. Here the basic elements of NIMS and its overall operational elements can be stressed and tested along with echelon challenges which entail working with state, federal and military augmentation and support.

Enhancing Resilience—often communities have benefited from prior investments in hardening those areas where vulnerabilities and risks are greatest but this exercise features renewed focus on upgrading mitigation measures and further risk reduction actions. Experts on selected infrastructural issues, industrial operations, schools and sensitive sites can offer ways to enhance resilience through well-structured tabletops where a differential threat scenarios are examined.

School Emergencies—the idea here would be to explore threat scenarios and emergencies which go beyond the "active shooter" environment and determine how schools would perform in emergencies where adverse weather, proximate hazmat events, or natural disasters required school officials to deploy their EOPs and observe how differential public safety support and coordination efforts would actually unfold. Along with this area of exercise planning is joint and collaborative work with local colleges and universities to ensure that areas of concern and substantial risk are well understood.

Terrorism—in this instance the focus could be either on a direct terrorist attack in the community or the residual set of complex emergency issues arising from a terror attack in a nearby community where residents and travelers would relocate, evacuate or temporarily seek shelter in what they felt was a safe location. Such an exercise can explore diverse scenarios which can range from cyber to actual explosive attacks and it can feature not only how local emergency responders would deal with a terror event but also how terror events in the nearby area might trigger new demands on the community. CBRNE events could also feature how military support elements might participate in emergency response.

Mass Casualty Events—many communities lack a solid grasp of how prepared their regional or local public health system is for a mass casualty event, which is defined as one where at least 300 simultaneous casualties requiring some form of hospitalization occurs or where an emergency happens, and the number of casualties far exceeds the capacity of local public health facilities to accommodate the demand. Again, the introduction of military augmentation assets and support could also be explored.

Mega-Disasters—the driving forces for this set of exercises would be to explore the farthest edges of expectable natural disasters such as floods, quakes, hurricanes and tornados to review and examine how disasters at the outer fringe of likelihood (F-4 tornados, 7.9 quakes, 200 year floods) would adversely affect communities, overstress EMACs and curtail the extent to which federal and state assistance could be provided. The aim here is to take a look at how local community first responders would behave in scenarios that are burdensome, complex and that far exceed ordinary expectations.

Grid Collapse—U.S. government policy requires a stern look at grid collapse scenarios where power is lost for a considerable period of time in excess of three weeks and where cascading effects featuring progressive loss of food, pharmacy, medical, fuel and supplies would be gradually degraded. In many local communities there is hardly a robust strategy for dealing with such outages and yet emergency first responders must reckon with the risk that triggering disruptive events such as solar storms, cyber attack, terrorism, or industrial accident could invite the onset of this crisis.

Agrosecurity Crises—one aspect of emergency planning which often goes overlooked is the vast agrosecurity infrastructure which spans the set of problematic issues from farm to table. This includes well-being of livestock, protection of vital grains and vegetables, manufacturing safety standards for food processing, and a number of other key elements in the overall food harvest, delivery, and storage system apart from retail and neighborhood grocers. Concerns about disease, food safety, and security as well as safeguarding agricultural imports and related products from tampering or terrorism must be included.

Soft Target Attacks—while we often assume that sporting events, large shopping malls and county fairs seem unlikely targets of attack and terrorism we must contemplate the risks which may attach to these events where state and federal assistance will be provided at leats seventy-two hours after the damage has been done. Most local communities are simply not prepared for the first seventy-two hours after such an attack and these situations must be part of any coherent EOP.

Post Disaster Rebuild—an area that is fraught with faulty assumptions and misleading information is the extent to which a local community has truly planned through the first five weeks of post disaster rebuild and recovery activities. Sometimes these events are regrettably take for granted owing to the fatal belief that FEMA assistance teams will carry the bulk of work to be done. Instead communities must delve deeply into the expectations, constraints, and opportunities which arise in disaster's aftermath.

Unified Command Events—the emphasis in this examination of exercise dynamics is to better understand how layered federal oversight and coordination of major disasters would actually operate along with reviews of the interagency dynamics and demands which a unified command structure imposes on local communities and emergency responders. This enables planners to estimate and identify the extent to which federal augmentation

Figure 8.2 Key steps in structuring exercise evaluations.

actually enhances overall response and to identify where possible gaps in coordination might arise.

This short listing of possible new ventures in emergency exercises is intended to underscore the variety and depth of issues and challenges which today's emergency managers and planners must account for thereby ramping up overall community preparedness. Many more could be listed but these activities reflect a wide variety of issues intended to further enable communities of all sizes, risk dimensions, and incident histories to wrestle with some key recurrent matters that deserve serious consideration.

There is also much to recommend serious consideration of the Homeland Security Exercise and Evaluation Program (HSEEP) platform for engaging in enhanced exercise design activities. Exercise designers and planners must take advantage of FEMA's steady improvements to the HSEEP process and the value it imparts to those who use it. The purpose of the HSEEP is to provide a national standard for exercises. This standard is based on capabilities-based planning and emphasizes the need to build capabilities suitable for responding to a wide range of hazards. HSEEP provides consistent terminology and tools for all exercise planners. Although these features are standardized, HSEEP can be applied to the full spectrum of hazardous scenarios and incidents.

The overall HSEEP process has evolved since 2007 into a more sophisticated mechanism to assist local community emergency planners with a better perspective on building credible exercises. While the FEMA website offers more direct instruction the HSEEP process has eight principal steps:

Analysis of the above FEMA diagram is intended to highlight the value of each suggested step. The first four steps of the process address evaluation planning, observation, and analysis. Such steps are fairly routine yet they require some careful consideration as they provide a foundation for the next four steps which follow. Here the results reflected in the AAR and the related improvement plan can make a real difference in enhanced response operations.

1. Plan and Organize the Evaluation: Step 1 is part of the exercise design process. In it, the Exercise Planning Team determines what information to collect, who will collect it, and how it will be collected.
2. Observe the Exercise and Collect Data: Step 2 occurs during the exercise. In it, expert evaluators collect data and record observations. They also collect data from records and logs.
3. Analyze Data: During Step 3, evaluators use Exercise Evaluation Guides (EEGs) to analyze data and reconstruct exercise events.
4. Develop the Draft After-Action Report: In Step 4, the Evaluation Team develops the draft After-Action Report (AAR). It describes what happened in the exercise, issues to be addressed, best practices, and recommendations for improvement.

   While these fundamental steps launch the HSEEP process with a ficus on exercise evaluation the second four steps of the process are detailed below. These steps focus on using information gained from exercises to implement improvements to a jurisdiction's capabilities.
5. Conduct an After-Action Conference: In Step 5, evaluators, participating agency representatives, and senior officials attend an After-Action Conference. Its purpose is to review the draft After-Action Report (AAR), define actions agencies can take to improve performance, and validate recommendations.
6. Identify Improvements to be Implemented: During the After-Action Conference, attendees identify corrective actions that address the areas for improvement and recommendations listed in the draft AAR. These corrective actions are captured on the Improvement Plan (IP).
7. Finalize the After-Action Report/Improvement Plan (AAR/IP): In Step 7, the exercise planning and evaluation teams incorporate corrections, clarifications, and other participant feedback into the AAR/IP.
8. Track Implementation: In Step 8, each agency or jurisdiction monitors corrective actions identified in the finalized AAR/IP.

As FEMA points out on its own website the information gleaned from this process has to be redirected toward real improvements in overall operational performance. The jurisdiction's work is not done when it has completed these eight steps. Long after the exercise is over, the jurisdiction's program managers will track and analyze the implementation of corrective actions listed in the After-Action Report/Improvement Plan (AAR/IP). By tracking and recording progress on corrective actions, the jurisdiction engages in a continuous Corrective Action Program (CAP). Through the CAP, the implementation of corrective actions leads to concrete improvements to preparedness.

When working with private sector industrial activities where latent risks of accident, systems failure, natural disaster or terror attack results in dangerous or toxic releases which jeopardize the immediate environment and nearby communities. Petroleum refineries, chemical plants, fertilizer plants, and related industrial operations of a high risk nature require special attention not only because local communities must closely coordinate emergency response operations with the facility safety and security officer, nut because facility managers must understand what the capacity of local emergency responders may be to the array of technical risks posed.

Areas for potential scrutiny include overall site mitigation strategies, containment venting options, seismic risk evaluations, flood hazard studies, power loss emergencies, control station blackout situations, community notification, and staged evacuation issues. For more complex situations like nuclear plants, or laboratories where dangerous pathogens may escape, emergency managers must devise plans which take into account the risk variables involved. In both cases an EPZ (emergency planning zone) must be devised along with an area risk map which displays areas of relative safety, exclusion zones, containment zones, and locations where emergency leadership can securely manage any incident.

One assumption which deserves repetition is the notion that future exercises always build on the results of prior exercises and take into account new requirements, unique threats, untested capabilities, and revised EOPs. New issues and challenges can be embedded in these areas which are not well-known until or unless a well-crafted exercise brings them to light. With that goes the caveat that novel approaches to exercise evaluation should also receive favorable consideration. Interviews, film clips, and message analysis, pinpointing areas of effective and ineffective communication or coordination and how unexpected setbacks and roadblocks are overcome deserve prominence in any new exercise evaluation scheme.

Finally, obstacles to onward and regularized emergency exercises must be confronted and overcome. There are always budgetary obstacles, equipment and personnel obstacles, leadership and political support problems as well as certain degrees of reluctance to engage repeatedly in exercises. Claims that costs are too high, that insufficient numbers of key players cannot be assembled, risks that an exercises might reveal an operational shortfall that nobody wants to expose, or that the exercise deals with a low probability yet high impact event have to be confronted. If a proposed exercise that is well-structured and realistic is rejected early on based upon claims that it is highly unlikely or extreme the community and its leaders must reckon with the possibility that failure to prepare for a unique emergency scenario renders the community dangerously vulnerable. Exercises which simply repeat prior exercises, focus on routine risks and stay within safe zones of expected performance are of limited value. Reaching out to test, stress and sustain operations in ways which require a response to demanding conditions are always better than repeating operations that are well-known.

These areas of consideration are not meant to be all inclusive. They simply suggest places where potential hazard planning and standby response strategies can be developed. Communities and proximate industrial sites must allow for modified emergency exercises such as tabletops to examine the central risk and hazard analysis issues involved. It is also recommended that local universities be afforded the opportunity to conduct cooperative research on risk mitigation, hazard assessment, emergency response, EMAC issues and leadership variables to pinpoint useful domains of interest in shaping a more effective crisis response structure. Colleges with substantial emergency management degree-granting programs can help capture useful data extracted from case studies where largely similar situations have been successfully dealt with elsewhere.

QUESTIONS

1. What is the value and significance of using HSEEP resources in exercise design?
2. Why does it make sense to consider COOP and infrastructure exercises as an alternative?
3. What is the advantage of working with military organizations in exercise planning

RESEARCH ACTIVITIES

1. How has your community decided to deal with extended grid collapse emergencies?
2. What have local emergency planners set up in coordinated response operations with business leaders?
3. How has your community availed itself of HSEEP resources?

Chapter 9

Adding Complexity and Challenge to Exercise Design

Almost 20 years ago a small group of national security experts convened in Washington to assess the widest variety of likely threats facing the USA in consideration of the damage and strategic surprise we endured during the infamous 9-11 attacks. The overall effort was to look into the future about five years or more and determine what feasible and likely threats might be at our nation's doorstep and which would contain elements of strategic surprise or significant damage to our security. At the time we generated 15 planning scenarios which included major natural disasters like earthquakes and hurricanes but we also injected scenarios involving chemical attacks, bio-attacks, radiological attacks and nuclear detonations. In that spectrum of issues we inadvertently expanded the scope and direction of national policy and prodded many federal, state and local agencies and emergency officials to take these scenarios seriously. Those 15 scenarios drove planning, technology development, preparedness training, emergency response dynamics and countless ventures to sharpen federal, state and local capabilities to respond effectively in the event one of those dire scenarios ever happened. It launched a nationwide procurement and planning effort to acquire and develop the innate capacity to respond to the full range of the 15 scenarios depicted and assess the mix of federal, state, and local resources needed to respond.[1]

Years and millions of dollars were invested in extensive preparations since 2002 to fulfill the response capacity expected against some of the most devastating and complex scenario challenges such as a dirty bomb, biological attack, and equivalent mixes of CBRN and natural disasters which suggested a high risk of cascading and multiple catastrophes. That overall focus on highest level catastrophes ripe with complexities and major challenges characterized the group effort—of which I was a part—to focus our nation on enhanced preparedness. There were few illusions that this would be easy as the budgetary and technology trade offs were already underway as increased optempo in our military response to 9-11 was placed alongside a multiyear program of enhanced domestic readiness. Just like the military campaign against Al-Qaeda and international terrorism, the domestic upsurge in building response capacity for the 15 scenarios rivaled that national warfare resolve in terms of dollars and resources invested in raising the bar on emergency response.

Long since then we have had to grapple with substantive and structural demands that we further diversify and upgrade emergency response capabilities for a wider range of crisis contingencies. Since the dawn of the twenty-first century we have redirected energy, creativity, budgets, technology development and emergency response operational doctrine into areas of enhanced CBRN readiness, better mass casualty preparedness, more coordinated deployment of military defense support elements to buttress state and local government activities and we have turned our attention to confront cyber, urban terrorist and high tech vulnerabilities. This has ushered in an era of wider sophistication and nuanced attention to scenarios which reflect the risk spectrum of our times and refocus our imaginations on the degree to which threat, risk and crisis scenarios of the future will grow in intensity and complexity. Hence, our primary shift in priority must be toward the edges of the risk bell curve to address unexpected, technologically complex and multifaceted emergencies.

While fundamental exercise design principles and structural concerns remain fairly constant and reflect boilerplate standards which merit continuation our compelling challenges in emergency exercise design involve going beyond the 15 national planning scenarios and those new scenarios we have added during the last 20 years. To be more specific, and set the stage for this new chapter, the call for much greater attention to be paid to several issues of future significance because they entail complex challenges laden with catastrophe . . .

- we need to do a better job of public warning [massive fires, CBRN attack, pandemics]
- we need to do better using the full potential of social media for response and recovery
- we need to be more sophisticated about the range of newer and complex CBRN threats
- we need to grasp how different outlier [black swan] emergencies are versus ordinary crises
- we need to better prepare for scenarios where the 'maximum of maximum' disaster looms
- we need to pay serious attention to managing mixed agrosecurity and public health crises

- we need to better manage novel pandemics and outbreaks of unknown deadly diseases
- we need better collective federal, state and local strategies for major cyber attacks
- we need to build real business continuity strategies in partnership with emergency experts
- we need better collaboration between urban and university emergency managers
- we need better federal, state, and local strategies to deal with long term grid collapse issues
- we need a better grasp of risk, threats, and challenges of future complex catastrophes

In many ways, this is only a preliminary agenda for the onward evolution and growth of emergency management as a profession. The decade beginning in 2020 will be severely complex compared to today's emergency issues, and those we traditionally prepare for, as subtly nuanced risks arise in areas of emerging disease research, mixes of advanced dual use technology, increased lateral and indirect cyber vulnerabilities and many others which are only dimly recognized now. There are far too many issues and related problems which devolve from these probing questions. They merit increased university and professional research and study because they will always be seen as simply rhetorical matters until they are thoroughly examined. The remainder of the twenty-first century will affirm that routine neglect and avoidance of answering these questions will lead to greater operational problems and performance shortfalls in years to come.

The central message here is that after 2020 FEMA-led National Exercises need to be expanded in scope and focus to embrace the complex, the unexpected, and the out of the box challenges and emphasize the multidimensional nature of future disasters. Failing this advise we absorb a higher risk of failure and mistaken operational alternatives if we don't lean into the array of suspected novel and complex scenarios ahead of us.

RECKONING THE VALUE OF NATIONAL EXERCISES

National exercises led and designed by the Federal Emergency Management Agency (FEMA) provide a glimpse into the federal, state and local partnership for dealing with major emergency events. Sometimes they reflect the most pressing security and emergency preparedness gaps we need to address and sometimes they hover over fairly routine disasters where changes in doctrine or policy must be tested. No doubt, one can focus entirely on the themes and issues which FEMA suggests each year in its major national exercise program and become fairly content with that. However, as we contemplate whether future scenarios will be inherently more complex, multidimensional and far reaching we may find that fails to satisfy. It makes sense to ask whether that FEMA trend line of National Level Exercises (NLEs) sufficiently stretches, improves and challenges people who have acquired five or more years dealing with a range of emergencies. Does it present novel issues, unexpected challenges and intractable conundrums which have seldom been encountered before? What matters most is whether typical urban police, fire, EMT and emergency staff feel adequately trained, equipped and prepared for major catastrophes which may overwhelm their cadre and trigger widespread and prolonged disruption to normal life. In effect we are asking whether the skills and tactics adequate to the past and the familiar are adequate to the future and what it may unleash.

This is much more than issuing a caution about retaining a false sense of security, or chastening emergency departments that have grown weary of the same old emergency scenarios, or drawing attention to underutilized emergency staff and equipment. The central issue is whether the spectrum of ongoing chaotic, emergency, disaster and catastrophic events is sufficiently complex, disturbing and challenging enough to keep emergency leadership and staff on their toes and thereby buried in research and collaborative ventures to find pathways, solutions and interim fixes. In effect, this is a warning about growing soft and ignoring the array of twenty-first century risks and challenges which our urban and rural emergency leadership will face. Declining budgets, staff cuts, and postponed investments in technology aside—this is a call to reflect and review whether today's emergency experts feel they are prepared, trained and equipped for the most dangerous, insoluble, complex and comprehensively devastating emergencies the future can deliver.

FEMA conducted its NLE 2018 bringing together more than 12,000 individuals from all levels of government, private industry, and nongovernmental organizations to protect against, respond to, and recover from a major Mid-Atlantic hurricane. The NLEO was scheduled during the first two weeks of May and provided a unique chance to examine lessons from Hurricanes Harvey, Irma, and Maria. The overall thrust of the national exercise was build on the insights of 2017 in order to improve operations and coordination across all levels of government, the private sector, and the public in advance of the concerns attached to the 2018 hurricane season. The exercise scenario involved a major hurricane that made landfall near Hampton Roads, Virginia, causing severe damage to residences, businesses, and critical infrastructure throughout the Mid-Atlantic. Fictional Hurricane Cora included power outages and cascading effects, with impacts to communications, transportation, water, and public works.[2]

There is nothing inherently wrong or misguided about reviewing the significant threats which hurricanes symbolize with an eye toward ramping up coordination and enhancing response. It makes sense to do this and take account of the fact that hurricanes are seasonal and recurrent and often pack a devastating punch for affected areas. Notice that the same national exercise in 2018 was far different than the same event four years earlier.

When comparing the 2018 NLE with a capstone national exercise in 2014, we find that the exercise was aimed primarily at enabling Federal stakeholders to demonstrate operational coordination and information sharing capabilities with the private sector and other non-traditional partners. There was also a major untried effort to make the 2014 exercise multidimensional and complex such as discerning whether this mixed collaborative team could engage in and fulfill internal damage assessments to validate capabilities, pinpoint urgent needs and identify key issues or potential shortfalls. *The 2014 scheme by FEMA featured five multiple requirements which included:*

1. Alaska Shield sponsored by the State of Alaska to commemorate the 50th anniversary of the 1964 Great Alaskan Earthquake providing central scenario elements: significant damage from both the quake and the tsunami it triggers will affect the greater Pacific Northwest placing demands in the federal interagency and the state to educate and prepare the whole emergency response community for complex, large-scale disasters and emergencies

2. Ardent Sentry was included to test Department of Defense readiness to perform its full scope Defense Support to Civilian Authorities' mission.

3. A Nuclear Weapon Accident/Incident Exercise (NUWAIX) was also included as a simultaneous crisis which features an accident during secure transportation of a nuclear weapons convoy in southwestern United States. Intelligence and national leadership will be tasked in the exercise to quickly determine the cause and significance of the accident.

4. A fourth add on to the 2014 exercise was tagged as Eagle Horizon 2014 which focuses on continuity of operations and reconstitution planning, requiring Federal departments and agencies to activate continuity plans and perform their Primary Mission Essential Functions from their alternate facilities

5. FEMA's fifth add on exercise element was called Silver Phoenix which merged operational with and discussion-based activities to examine the full range of recovery efforts and operations commencing upon the notification that a catastrophic incident has occurred.

Clearly, FEMA has made efforts in 2014 to magnify the complexity and diversity of urgent scenarios while underscoring the criticality and chaos of simultaneous disasters brimming with divergent dangers and calamity. As such, the 2014 exercises tried to explore the challenges associated with multiple geographically dispersed disasters while examining, prioritizing, and conducting recovery activities involving those dispersed and competing events using the National Disaster Recovery Framework.[3]

That enterprise was a laudable goal and impressive in its sweep and scope. However, whether the mix of five events in 2014 did the trick and actually enhanced our national capacity to respond effectively to simultaneous disasters of significant difficulty is anyone's guess. Those who actually participated were convinced this scenario mix would bring conventional government operations and leadership to a halt. Maybe new insights and better fits of technology and skilled cadre were discovered. The suggestion here is that we need to apply imagination, foresight and creativity to shape the future national emergency response enterprise for issues, threats and disasters after 2020.

What always undermines exercises of this scope and political sensitivity is whether actual shortfalls and lapses in response operations are identified and surfaced for remedial action in after action reports. There is often a disturbing tendency to sweep aside errors and operational mistakes in favor of a resounding report that all went well—or just as planned.

Overall happiness, satisfaction and professional reinforcement of skills and technology after a national exercise is healthy however benign neglect of tough issues and complex surprises lurking inside unanswered operational questions is not. Exercise happiness cannot overcome robust improvement.

One salient question about the 2014 exercise is a need to report and summarize publicly what agency actions, innovations, breakthroughs and gestures went well and isolate those aspects which remain troubling, unsolved or problematic. Captured in the minds of players and observers who were there is the complete story about what went right, what went wrong, and what surprised everyone during the 2014 NLE. To some extent the full story will be hard to get. Takeaways from that seminal event are likely still nascent and somewhat unclear even today as the central dilemma of rationing national emergency leadership among five simultaneous tragedies and balancing national security interests against ongoing domestic catastrophes symbolizes a scenario we have not deeply explored.

Without doubt this was a risky venture and those who participated in the 2014 NLE shared mixed reviews of its success and beneficial outcomes. While FEMA deserves credit for trying to create a complex and challenging catastrophe the question is whether they actually did so. Adding complexity and challenge to exercise design, especially when multiple simultaneous catastrophes occur, is worth exploring continually and annually. It forces emergency planners, leaders and expert responders to deal with issues and problems they have never faced before. It adds a depth of technical, substantive and subtly confounding complexity and forces consideration of novel, untried and largely experimental avenues for finding fixes and interim solutions. It painstakingly requires new thinking, creative assessments, approaches outside the realm of comfortable perception and serious consideration of random mayhem. This begs the question of whether national level exercises, which are costly and devour thousands of planning hours, ought to be focused on complex and challenging catastrophes every year and feature multiple simultaneous disasters.

EXERCISING ANNUAL COMPLEX, CHALLENGING, CATASTROPHES

It may seem obvious that there is merit to devoting FEMA's limited annual resources on exercises which delve into prior events and assess what new insights and lessons can be derived from them as they did in 2018. Again, there is also merit in exploring the issues and dynamics which a complex exercises like that unleashed in 2014 deserves serious consideration. The take away from this apparent trade-off is to determine the net value of both events to participants, the interagency players and those ostensibly deriving benefits well after the NLE is finished and the after action report filed.

There is also merit in determining whether we actually know enough about the many specific discrete and unexpected issues which did arise in Alaska Shield, NUWAIX, Ardent Sentry and Eagle Horizon. In some cases each of these sub exercises contained a wealth of problems and revelations entirely within the scenario not likely seen before in handling each event, let alone the urgent conflicts and trade-offs which likely arose as federal unified commanders had to balance one crisis and its demands against the others. In that sense the argument for NLE events which add complexity and multiple catastrophes is compelling.

However, we also understand the value that the 2018 NLE must have conveyed to those taking a deeper look at a collection of catastrophic hurricanes and delineating what the key ideas and challenges were. That, by itself, seems equally compelling. So we are left to wonder whether choosing one NLE framework over another seems persuasive. In many ways it does not. Emphasizing one legitimate scenario framework to the exclusion or postponement of the other risks loss of corporate response and recovery memory, erosion of operational insights and dilution of emergency management knowledge. From a national standpoint where FEMA seeks to build and reinforce expertise and interagency collaboration between the government and the private sector, or explore defense support issues and CBRN response problems, the losses outweigh the benefits. We can safely inquire whether the full spectrum of obvious and subtle insights were gleaned by national leadership from that event.

The range of unexpected, complex and challenging exercise scenarios is virtually limitless. Runaway pandemics with raging communicable diseases of unknown origin, radiological meltdown of several coastal nuclear reactors, or a random EMP or solar storm knocking out 65 percent of our national grid, all reflect catastrophic situations where national exercises should redirect emphasis and stay committed year after year until solid and reliable answers are found. Complex catastrophes cannot dwell any longer at the extreme edges of the bell curve of disaster probability. They deserve to be front and center and the eternal focus of serious researchers and leaders in emergency management. They cannot be easily neglected.

One valid take away is that in alternate years FEMA could seriously consider the 2014 multiple catastrophe scenario and in between years steer experts to review persistent natural disasters such as hurricanes, quakes, wild-fires and floods. In this alternate years approach the NLE has a better chance of reinforcing the collective and collaborative skill sets and technologies which must be deployed to reckon with well known and unexpected crises.

DETERMINING RISKS, THREATS, HAZARDS AND THE UNEXPECTED

Consideration ought be given to a sweeping approach to emergency exercise design for the remainder of the twenty-first century which embraces, invites and incorporates scenarios that are inherently complex, difficult and challenging. This avenue toward more comprehensive exercise planning is what I call *the HURT paradigm*. HURT reflects emphasis on hazards, unexpected events, rigorous risk analysis, and out of the box assessment of threats. HURT automatically calls for a strict inventory of response capabilities that is calibrated to the relative percentage of problem resolution and crisis containment. In effect it draws attention to a sliding scale of emergency response readiness based on the inherent complexity and challenge of the specific emergency scenario being faced.

The exemplar or archetype for risk and hazard analysis can be chosen from a variety of methods and approaches many of which have been validated and time tested. Conventional risks analysis draws from literally hundreds of methods and theories each of which has its own persuasive value and drawbacks. Risk assessment by itself doesn't get emergency managers closer to genuine understanding of what they worry about most—unexpected crises, overwhelming broad scope demands, and limited tools and operational strategies to wrestle the disaster to the ground.

Table 9.1 HURT Paradigm Index

Intensity Index	Hazards	Unexpected Events	Rigourous Risk Analysis	Out of Box Threats
Level 1	Minor	Very Unlimited	Traditional	Few Identified
Level 2	Moderate	Limited	Revised	Some Identified
Level 3	Major	Significant	Original	Many Identified

What is needed is another approach that may reveal more insights and information about the unexpected and out of the box disasters that can plague cities and communities. The HURT paradigm is no different in that it merely suggests another alternative avenue for assessing what the seen and unseen aspects of a risk evaluation ought include.

What the chart displays is a mixture of conventional and unconventional methods for assessing risks, threats and hazards in ways which may augment exercise planning efforts.

One approach is to consider Level 1 activities as the kind of ordinary emergency exercises that perhaps 80 percent of our major cities and states engage in on a regular basis. These exercise only affirm, test and validate existing capabilities and staff is seldom pushed to manage and consider more complex factors embedded in the simulation. Level 2 increases the sheer number and variety of hazards, adds a number of unexpected events which are plausible, forces new thinking about the scope an adequacy of risk analysis, and tackles the appearance of 'out of the box' threats unanticipated, cascading, inadvertent and random in nature. When you devise an exercises at Level 3 you are deliberately taxing and stressing the emergency team to handle upper tier problems far beyond the conventional and ordinary with clear inclusion of catastrophic dynamics and consideration of 'maximum of maximum' scenarios.

Some recent examples of this include the runaway California wildfires in 2018 which clearly overtaxed firefighters, emergency responders and other experts as homes, businesses and people surrendered to greater loss and jeopardy than ever before. The actual crisis far exceeded the plans, preparations and assumptions which emergency leadership invested in their preparations and evidenced scenarios where skilled staff were clearly overwhelmed. Likewise the dangerous and misleading false alarms issued by Hawaii scaring its population to expect a North Korean missile attack illustrates that the art and science of issuing accurate and timely warning messages contains a network of questions beyond human error that suggests more work is needed to avoid repeating that fiasco.

Adding complexity and challenge is the key to ramping up emergency leadership and response cadre readiness for catastrophic scenarios which are often ignored or avoided for budgetary reasons, leadership hesitancy or because the prospect of partial or significant failure among participants would be embarrassing to exercises players. A dismal fact long verified by those who have designed, witnessed and evaluated many federal level exercises. Readiness to deal with what is termed 'black swan's or 'outlier' issues in the realm of the unexpected, unknown and untried must become the new basic standard for emergency exercises otherwise we may deceive ourselves about the true response capacity we assume we possess.

CONSIDERING THE INTERNATIONAL EXERCISE PERSPECTIVE

Another factor in designing emergency exercises beyond 2020 involves reckoning with emerging international concepts of risk and hazard which have never been systematically compared or reconciled with the way problems are managed in the USA. Two such examples are the kinds of principles and issues which OECD and the UN view as essential and significant. These foreign institutions may be more reliant on disaster modeling than here in the USA but their approach merits a closer look. One related issue is the degree to which academic institutions which promote degree programs in emergency management actually collaborate with genuine emergency managers to make their programs and curriculum more relevant and pragmatic. Seldom does that collaboration take place.

For example the OECD stresses the importance of distinguishing between deterministic and probabilistic scenarios and implies that subtle influences like this shape and steer exercise design considerations. In addition, the UN reinforces the significance of using these two versions of scenario construction with additional emphasis on the importance of actually modeling these diverse scenarios as a way of validating emergency response capabilities.

Deterministic risk considers the impact of a single risk scenario, whereas probabilistic risk considers all possible scenarios, their likelihood and associated impacts. Deterministic approaches are used to assess disaster impacts of a given hazard scenario, whereas probabilistic methods are used to obtain more refined estimates of hazard frequencies and damages. Probabilistic assessments are characterized by inherent uncertainties, partly related to the natural randomness of hazards, and partly because of our incomplete understanding and measurement of the hazards, exposure and vulnerability under consideration[4]

While historical losses can explain the past, they do not necessarily provide a good guide to the future; most disasters that could happen have not happened yet (UNISDR, 2013a). Probabilistic risk assessment simulates those future disasters which, based on scientific evidence, are likely to occur (UNISDR, 2015). As a result, these risk assessments resolve the problem posed by the limits of historical data (UNISDR, 2015). Probabilistic models therefore "complete" historical records by reproducing the physics of the phenomena and recreating the intensity of a large number of synthetic events (UNISDR, 2015).

In contrast, a deterministic model treats the probability of an event as finite. The deterministic approach typically models scenarios, where the input values are known and the outcome is observed. There is overlap in deterministic and probabilistic modelling. For example, probabilistic modelling (i.e. running multiple scenarios at different probabilities of occurrence) can be used to generate a deterministic scenario; typical scenarios might include:[5]

- Worst-case *e.g. the maximum losses*
- Best-case e.g. the losses that can be absorbed
- Most "likely" e.g. the losses that are most likely to occur

The OECD and UN approaches are worth examining but we must also direct serious attention to another related hurdle which will delineate the difference between classical and conventional emergency exercise planning and what we need for future threats, hazards and risks. It is a serious excursion into the realm of 'maximum of maximum' [MOM]scenarios which approximates the scope, complexity, uncertainty and difficulty of truly catastrophic crises and which pointedly challenge emergency management leadership, experts and responders in ways which elevate their overall readiness.

Some years ago FEMA hosted what it termed a "maximum of maximum' [or MOM] tabletop exercises which appeared to mix several parallel and cascading emergencies beginning with a Category 4 hurricane followed by massive flooding and extended power outage. It was a fine example of a staged MOM event but failed to push players and agencies far beyond their comfort level and may have fallen short of presenting a challenge seen by players as truly overwhelming and catastrophic. This may have been an opening gambit to add vertical and horizontal complexity to a national exercise.

FEMA may have been trying to broach the issue of a genuine doomsday scenario and term its efforts as Maximum of Maximums emergency exercises. This may be because FEMA itself, coined the MOM activity which typically includes a small universe of mixed disaster possibilities—a major hurricane, a major earthquake, or an improvised nuclear device. This is reasonable to an extent but still falls short of mixing more complex scenarios which include genuine top level challenges. One example for consideration is this MOM scenario:

A dirty bomb exploding proximate to the end of the Houston Ship Channel, in conjunction with mortar explosions along IH-37 petrochemical facilities triggering toxic leaks, followed by cyber attacks on energy, chemical and petroleum complexes adjacent to Houston and triggering a massive power outage, thousands of casualties and a radiologically compromised emergency response zone. Commercial shipping into and out of Houston, and onward refining and distribution of crude oil is interrupted, as geographically dispersed mass casualty situations arise in La Marque, Texas City, Houston and the IH-37 corridor.

In some ways this is the lower end of plausible MOM scenarios as it blends CBRN, mass casualty, toxic jeopardy, FBI terrorism response coordination, commercial disruption, damage containment, urban evacuation and site stabilization challenges and many might speculate that its largely local orientation makes it manageable by a unified command scheme. This MOM scenario implies the risk of future spatially dispersed secondary attacks alongside the urgent need for immediate relief and response. It takes imagination and a serious appreciation for the array of blended terrorism and national security threats we face to consider whether we have the deployable emergency response enterprise we need today for this MOM event. What federal interagency leadership entity makes that call? If we don't—we certainly need it soon.

Coupling natural disasters with subsequent and cascading technological, natural and other disasters is the starting point for exercises designers who want to challenge their leadership and response staff. Starting with the massive Fukushima disaster in Japan and moving upwards from there in sheer complexity and variety of secondary emergencies toward catastrophic events where mass casualty demands exceed 20,000 victims, military augmentation to civil authorities lacks the requisite technologies or personnel or where wildly diverse evacuation patterns wreck havoc with staged relief and recovery operations. These are the situations and circumstances that must be tested and explored.

Sophisticated scenarios for the remainder of the 21st century must delve into the unexpected, the complex, the difficult and the catastrophic. We cannot devise coherent and relevant emergency policy, test and validate emergency collaboration procedures, proof test new technology or verify the value and risks of onward technology-human systems without it.

Deliberate efforts to explore MOM scenarios, explore the dynamics of black swan events, and assess how our emergency response cadre performs under extended stress and duress situations will remain dangerously theoretical without these efforts.

By way of illustration here are two MOM scenarios which merit a closer look and suggest a need for sophisticated new approaches to conducting FEMA National Exercises. The first example features a 9.2 quake centered in southern California which opens the San Andreas fault and resonates 30 minutes later with an 8.4 quake 20 miles offshore west of Los Angeles near Huntingdon Beach. The third quake follows in 20 minutes with a 7.5 temblor 10 miles west of Lompoc and Vandenburg AFB. *The specific MOM scenario exemplar includes five major simultaneous crises all together requiring a federal response, unified command and post quake urban chaos.*

1. the initial 8.2 quake opens San Andreas fault splitting California in two for 164 miles
2. the second quake damages the San Onofre nuclear reactor releasing radioactivity
3. the third quake damages the Diablo Canyon nuclear reactor with core melt into the ocean
4. a tsunami with 30 ft waves targets the LA area for nearly 2 hours of incipient threat
5. quake damage to Vandenberg AFB results in toxic releases of nitrogen tetroxide on base

When we visualize the conventional hazard probability/severity risk grid that normally presents itself for observational validation we have to ask ourselves whether this chart adequately reflects the magnitude and complexity of this MOM scenario. If it does that's great—but if it doesn't what does that

Figure 9.1   San Onofre Reactor

Figure 9.2   Diablo Canyon Reactor

Figure 9.3   San Onofre Area Map

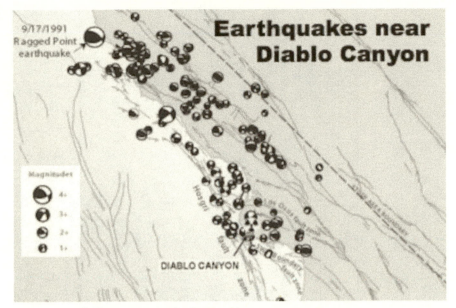

Figure 9.4 Diablo Canyon Quake Pattern Map

imply? If the scale, scope and metrics we use now to calibrate the severity and complexity of a disaster are less than accurate and adequate for the variety of complex future scenarios where does that leave us? In serious and complex MOM scenarios we have to contemplate whether a simplified matrix chart like this covers the depth and uncertainty shrouded within the triple quake scenario and cascading secondary emergencies assumed or described.

Another MOM scenario which merits attention may not have as many direct layers of complexity involves a legitimate future risk and its undeniably complex onward secondary effects. Here the mix of suspect terrorism, state sponsored hostility, and multidimensional domestic chaos ensues.

At 9:45pm EST in September 2020, the much feared risk of a surprise hostile EMP attack becomes a reality. Origins of the missile delivered nuclear detonation are vague and indistinct. While the White House devises military responses and tries to pinpoint the source of the attacks, the initial damage is done. The event features a small nuclear weapon detonated at a height sufficient to create the widest possible destructive footprint extending from Canada to Mexico and from the east to west coasts. Immediately all communications, computer enabled systems, electronics of all types, commercial aviation and motor vehicles are frozen and inoperable. In turn, water, power, commercial support systems, and secondary infrastructure failures multiply within minutes after the detonation. Cities east of the Rockies are in darkness and multiple zones of urban panic and chaos are unleashed.

Table 9.2 Coventional Risk Analysis Grid

		Hazard Probability				
		Frequent (A)	Probable (B)	Occasional (c)	Remote (D)	Improbable (E)
Single item		Likely to occur frequently	Will occur several times over life of item	Likely to occur sometime during life of item	Unlikely, but possible to occur during life of item	So unlikely, can assume occurrence to take place
Fleet/inventory		Occurs continuously	Will occur frequently	Will occur several times	Unlikely but reasonably expected to occur	Unlikely to occur, but possible
CATASTROPHIC (death or system loss)	I	High	High	High	High	Medium
CRITICAL (severe injury or occupational illness or major damage)	II	High	High	High	Medium	Low
MARGINAL (minor injury or ocupational illness or minor damage)	III	High	Medium	Medium	Low	Low
NEGLIGIBLE (less than minor injury, illness, or damage)	IV	Medium	Low	Low	Low	Low

Hazard Severity

Again, the mix of national security, terrorism, massive infrastructural failure, and crippled deployment and communications capabilities in the nationwide first responder community adds the requisite complexity, challenges and catastrophic flavor to the scenario. Those who may argue this scenario is unlikely or highly speculative may have failed to reckon with at least 22 years of consecutive strategic warnings about our vulnerability to a covert EMP attack and the miserable and deadly consequences it triggers.

The map identified below illustrates below the scope and scale of such an attack with indirect and cascading infrastructure failures in energy, water, communications, and other key systems. The USA, Canada and parts of Mexico would be crippled and isolated without electricity and energy to power crucial systems, safety controls and restrictive access panels. The knockout effects to national security and emergency response command, control and communications would be catastrophic rendering many local and urban communities without the resources and technology needed to manage the crisis and offset pressures for wider chaos and damage.

So we are left with the disturbing reality that our conventional risk assessment mechanisms and hazard assessments paradigms may not be accurate or comprehensive enough. The real emphasis here is on future shifts and changes in the nature of the 'all hazards spectrum' which needs to be rethought in terms of the vastly more complex situation we face in a technology laden and

Figure 9.5   EMP Effects Map

Table 9.3   Alternative Conventional Risk Management Chart

RISK MANAGEMENT ASSESSMENT

Risk Management Step	Assessment		Comments
	Sustain	Improve	
BEFORE THE MISSION			
1. Most Importtant Hazards Identified?		X	Only the most sporadic hazards identified. Sporadic input.
2. Risk Level of Each Hazard Assessed?		X	Not included in mission analysis
3. Controls Developed & Residual Risk Determined?	X		Options were presented to reduce risk
4. Risk Decision Made for Selected COA?	X		Recommendations approved by BN CDR during decision brief
5. Hazards & Controls Clearly Communicated?	X		Controls briefed as part of opord
DURING THE MISSION			
6. Controls Implemented and Enforced?	X		Chain of command emphasis
AFTER THE MISSION			
7. Risk Management Effective?		X	No Documentation/AAR

energy dependent 21st century. Planning for worst case situations is normally expected in the emergency management business but the challenge of dealing realistically with MOM scenarios is they will only get worse. In point of fact, we need to study and assess whether charts like the one below remain useful and instructive.

This implies that new thinking and much more diversified analysis is warranted as we survey the emergency management landscape after 2020. Complex, challenging and catastrophic scenarios are not only warranted they are essential. Relying on older and more familiar exercises scenarios does not provide assurances that confidence in our response systems to a new and more challenging 'all hazards' spectrum should be affirmed. Today we need genuine strategies for

—nationwide or regional extended term grid collapse
—major pandemics involving novel diseases where CDC cannot isolate its cause
—multiple cascading natural disasters nested within legitimate MOM scale scenarios
—thoughtful international collaboration on best emergency response methods and tactics

The collection of disaster scenarios is fairly unlimited in diversity, damage and disruption with the implied challenge that we somehow possess the innate capacity to deal with every scenario imaginable in an effective and comprehensive manner. We know that is an illusion and a dangerous assumption that contains the seeds of genuine strategic destruction. Efforts to prepare first responders, emergency managers, experts and leaders for the fullest range of disasters from benign to catastrophic must be the imperative for the remainder of this century. Shrinking from that challenge fails to provide the security and safety which most Americans expect and deserve.

WRESTLING WITH WICKEDNESS: EXERCISES IN CATASTROPHIC RECOVERY

An area of legitimate inquiry which seldom gets explored is the complex and nuanced phases of disaster recovery with special emphasis on catastrophic recovery. It takes a mammoth amount of analysis to undertake a full scope inventory of all the tasks that must be completed, their appropriate sequencing or priority, as well as estimating the finish line for their effective completion and the standards to be used to build in a level of resilience against future crises. This is neither automatic nor intuitive because it begs the question of what scope, scale, focus and structure a genuine recovery campaign requires. Further we have to delineate carefully the material distinctions between urban recovery in a city like Los Angeles vs a state capitol like Sacramento vs a smaller but important regional community like Escondido California. Worse we have to slice the recovery task further and identify what priorities and crucial steps are involved in bringing back industrial, commercial and citizen services enterprises. We also have to tackle the unpleasant and challenging work of bringing back all crucial elements of infrastructure and regenerating the economic heartbeat and signature characteristics of a badly damaged urban area.

Issues and challenges embedded in this undertaking require pre disaster planning and an intensive effort to exercise the full multi-phased activities which lead to recovery and may entail hidden, subtle and unknown obstacles which impede smooth remedial actions. The multi-phased process of recovery which must be exercised include . . .

Recovery Assessment—includes a period of two to 6 weeks wherein leaders and experts assess which commercial, industrial, residential, infrastructural and community support services functions and organizations merit highest priority. This would include a preliminary estimate of the sequencing and resource demands expected.

Restoration Milestones—includes delineating, specifying, staggering and ordinally arranging the sector specific milestones which indicate that damaged systems are on a steady path toward full recovery. This implied a limited restoration period which reflects degrees of recovery from minimal, to moderate to fully recovered functional integrity and operation. This will differ based on the enterprise and the extensive nature of the enabling technology and specialized resources which may be required. For example, bringing a damaged water purification system back into normal service will logically differ significantly from shutting down or restoring nuclear power. This also merits a closer look at system interdependencies. In all likelihood the restoration of energy systems must precede the gradual restoration of other key infrastructural systems.

Recovery Operations—includes all final steps and completion of pending restoration operations which enable and support the full recovery of damaged systems, industries, commercial entities and related indicators of a return to post-disaster normal conditions. Implied with this phase is the building in of deeper more complex resilience measures to offset the risks of persistent vulnerability to periodically recurring disasters.

Emergency exercises which deal directly with all phases of recovery, including the obvious socio-political challenge of restoring dwellings, neighborhoods, workplaces, public safety and health organizations and reopened schools are crucial. Attaining a sense of wider public support and confidence in institutions will necessitate enormous investments of resources and skilled leadership.

All of the rudimentary and highly detailed aspects of recovery from catastrophic disasters cannot be easily replicated in an exercise setting as the genuine pressures of conflicting demands, public intolerance for delay, disruptions and setbacks in conducting restoration operations are merely superficial indicators of how difficult recovery—especially for a major city or state capitol—can be. However, it seems there can be no substitute for the value of a well-planned and orchestrated effort to exercise the full scope, breadth and complexity of urban recovery and grasp the deeper dilemmas and conundrums encountered as we contemplate how multiple cities damaged to a catastrophic degree can be simultaneously restored and recovered. To assume this will happen naturally, or follow a predictable and smooth path, is a deadly and dangerous position to take.

MOMS AND BOMBS: SOME FINAL OBSERVATIONS

Here we have argued the case for greater reliance on using MOM scenarios to sharpen and upgrade the skills and innovative energies of our emergency management leaders and experts. This runs the gamut from low level disasters which prove to be highly manageable to those CBRN events, spectacular natural disasters, cosmic scenarios like meteor strikes, nuclear plant meltdowns and EMP attacks which elude management or control. It has to be seen a different way. The range of exercise consideration for the 21st century can be viewed as a spectrum of challenges which span the *'bombs to MOMs' set of scenarios* wherein all manner of complex, technical, unforeseen, very difficult and mind-numbingly comprehensive catastrophes are built into the emergency exercise logic and everyday thinking of our urban and national leaders.

Training and equipping our emergency experts, leaders and first responders for the most comprehensive array of disasters we are likely to face from 2020 onward is fundamental. Focusing on the easy, the familiar, the manageable and the expected will not provide the level of readiness and emergency preparedness which the public expects. Pushing the limits of imagination and driving toward those problems and crises which are patently overwhelming seems best even if it carries a price tag that invokes fear and loathing among political leaders and keepers of the treasury. The losses we endure and absorb from a truly catastrophic event will dwarf any incremental investment in preparing for wicked MOM scenarios. The time is now to invest serious resources in planning for MOM events.

Setting the bar for future emergency exercises means that leadership must foster these changes in direction, governments must find the funds to sponsor and support these MOM scenarios and expert players must be willing to risk some degree of failure or setback because the expectation of 'complete success' is not likely to be high. Progressively more difficult, challenging and complex MOM scenarios, along with other future threats and risks identified in this chapter, are what is needed to bring our collective emergency management enterprise to a higher level of readiness and preparedness. To remain locked in repetitive, routine and conventional emergency scenarios as a training vehicle after 2020 is riskier than not conducting any exercises at all. Challenges to existing emergency management capacity and flexibility are needed to keep pace with an expanding spectrum of risks and hazards.

These issues will drive emergency exercise planning deeper into the 21st century and widen the scope and focus of what we understand emergency management entails. Determined efforts to acquire skills and insights about future MOM scenarios and equally complex challenges are sorely needed. In some respects it can change the profession itself if the true range of newest and more complex 'all hazards' scenarios is grasped and understood.

DISCUSSION QUESTIONS

1. What aspects of traditional and conventional emergency exercises seem inadequate to the challenges of complex and unexpected risks and hazards after 2020?
2. If the MOM scenario suggested still seems inadequate, what alternative emergency scenarios with complexity, uncertainty and catastrophic challenge should be considered?
3. If insufficient resources, political support, and lackluster leadership all combine to thwart MOM exercises what alternatives exist to sharpen emergency responders to the issues and scenarios we may face after 2020?
4. Discuss whether you agree or not with the suggested national exercise strategy of alternating bi-annually natural disaster exercises with MOM exercises for the FEMA led national exercise program.

YOU TRY IT—RESEARCH ISSUES

Prepare and design your own MOM scenario which deals with cascading infrastructure failure, multiple mass casualty incidents and mixes in plausible natural disasters.

Outline the HURT paradigm strategy for assessing a MOM scenario where a major pandemic where the offending disease remains a mystery but the FBI suspects the population has been subjected to a bioweapons attack.

NOTES

1. Planning Scenarios Executive Summaries. https://www.facs.org/~/media/files/quality programs/trauma/disaster

2. FEMA, National Level Exercise, 2018; https://www.fema.gov/nle

3. FEMA, National Exercise Program (NEP), National Level Exercise-Capstone Exercise 2014; https://www.fema.gov/media-library/assets/documents/90725

4. OECD, *Risk Assessment Guide, 2012*. Risk Governance-OECD. www.oecd.org. Directorate for Public Governance

5. *UNISDR ANNUAL REPORT 2016*. https://www.unisdr.org/files/52253_unisdr 2016annualreport.pdf

Chapter 10

Summing It Up

In this little book, we have tried to summarize the key elements in effective emergency exercise design and evaluation, drawing attention to those operational and structural areas that existing textbooks have forsaken. We have emphasized that for most communities, the adage *you're on your own for the first seventy-two hours after a disaster* sums up the key issue.

However we also understand the grim fact that some complex emergencies contain elements of severely challenging destruction and damage which may result in seeing state and federal assistance taking much longer than three days to reach the hardest hit areas. So serious efforts to grapple deliberately with more challenging crises is paramount. It bears repeating that preparedness for many emergencies is one thing while planning for actual recovery from disaster is quite another.

Developing a capacity to recover, to withstand and absorb the worst effects of any disaster and to emerge from it resolute to tackle the array of post-disaster issues facing you is the very essence of resilience. This is a quality we want to see in every town, village, and city, where emergency responders know that citizens are prepared to assist and coordinate in dealing with the aftermath of a disaster rather than simply provide hundreds of helpless and needy victims at the worst possible time.

We have stressed that when exercises are properly designed and structured, both *preparedness and readiness can be assessed and tested*. It has been emphasized that exercises must enable demonstration of essential emergency response skills, using both actual equipment and technologies, to re-create *as realistic a setting for emergency response performance as humanly possible*. It has been stated in firm and clear terms that the performance standards, criteria, and expected levels of emergency response behavior should be *calibrated to reflect the most effective degree of behavior possible*. We have

stressed that first responders appreciate exercises that challenge them and
help them refine their skills rather than those events that only affirm a basic
capability. Finally, we have noted that citizens, political leaders, and anyone
whose determination is strong to see their tax dollars used wisely will endorse
efforts to make exercises as realistic, challenging, and opera-tionally dynamic
as possible. Exercises provide a unique training event and a seldom seen
opportunity to physically prove an emergency response capability exists that
effectively diminishes or resolves the crisis.

In our first chapter we summarized the four primary purposes of an
exercise:

1. Validate the assumptions and procedures of the EOP
2. Help identify real gaps in vulnerability assessments and capability
   determinations
3. Enable verification of staff preparedness and training for all-hazard
   emergencies
4. Provide a realistic opportunity to verify emergency readiness

This is the central thrust and foundation for any emergency exercise. If
an exercise can demonstrate that it accomplished these four purposes, it has
proven its value to the community and the cadre of professional emergency
responders. Moreover, we have consistently drawn attention to the *dual value
of exercises that enable determinations to be made by external and objective
experts about a community's preparedness and readiness for all-hazard emergencies.* Along with that is the keystone imperative that effective emergency
exercises challenge, stress, and sharpen the overall skills and performance
quality of emergency responders. Nothing is as damaging or worthless as an
exercise that fails to levy realistic and burdensome demands on emergency
workers. This is yet another reason why some jurisdictions, despite the cost
and the headaches involved, should seriously consider small-scale no-notice
exercises to keep emergency responders sharp and prepared. They may also
do routine TTX's to test specific functions and pinpoint problems that they
can rectify quickly and at low cost. Then when they are ready for a full-scale
no-notice exercise there should be far fewer issues to fix and the major ones
will have greater justification for funding and support.

At this point, it is also crucial to note that the overwhelming tone and
purpose of this book has been to address the needs and concerns of local
communities, villages, counties, and many small cities with due regard for
situations where state assistance or intervention may be needed. *In that sense,
the emphasis in this book has been on natural disasters, hazmat disasters, and
major technological systems disasters rather than on terrorist attacks.* This
was a deliberate effort to differentiate the tasks and challenges of Incident

Command and those instances of Unified Command where local emergency responders would be supplemented by EMAC, multicounty or state resources. In cases where terrorism is suspected, of course, the FBI, the military, the Department of Homeland Security and other federal agencies will likely be involved in some way. This is also true of a mega-disaster like Hurricane Katrina or the California Northridge earthquake, where federal intervention and eventual leadership of a multi-tiered Unified Command scheme is all but certain when major cities, ports, airports, industrial areas, and sensitive sites are involved.

It is also of crucial importance that cities and communities which ordinarily would never contemplate the risks of a terror attack in their own backyards begin to assess the effects of such an attack on a proximate target within fifty miles of their jurisdiction. This is necessary for quite a few justifiable reasons:

1. terror attacks nearby trigger evacuations/migrations near you
2. expect EMAC demands to assist or augment targeted areas
3. relocated persons arrive with profound medical/survival needs
4. temporary stress demands on your own shelter/infrastructures
5. increased duty demands on local public safety staff

Again, the kinds of situations where thousands may relocate from a targeted area to your community can be rooted in CBRN attacks or terror attacks where those shifting to your area will seek shelter and perhaps prolonged sustainment. Proximate targets of a terror attack nearby include stadiums, shopping malls, military bases, crucial energy and infrastructure enterprises and seaports. It would be a serious mistake to assume that the risks of such an event would be so low as to be discounted as plausible by local emergency planners.

In this book we have also underscored the importance of finding skilled expertise in exercise design and evaluation to ensure that the essential issues to be examined and assessed are drawn out of the effort in careful and professional detail. We have stated in each of the chapters the importance of exercise design, scenario development, MSEL drafting, and specification of taskers and injects to test first responders. It has been emphasized that tests of the EOC itself are also necessary to validate EOPs and to verify the utility and performance of essential communications equipment. Testing EOC relationships, functions, leadership, and internal operations are critical aspects of emergency preparedness often taken for granted that must be exercised. We understand the importance of exercise design principles and fundamentals that enable the structure and operation of exercises to flow smoothly.

Exercise Design Objectives

- Confirm individual/team training (KSAs)
- Demonstrate key performance functions
- Verify man-technology interface/operations
- Assess problem-solving
- Examine response readiness metrics
- Observe extended/novel stress incidents
- Evaluate target capabilities
- Determine issues and areas for further tests

We grasp the significance of objectives and their relationship to establishing a coherent framework for all the activities that will occur. There is little doubt we appreciate the efforts and creative energy needed to lay out the entire vision, scheme, and plan for an exercise—especially the more complex full field-deployed versions we know so well. But even in the world of tabletops thought must be given to how to maximize the talent assembled and whether the tabletop actually answers key operational questions and settles controversies about certain ambiguities that players know will arise in actual crisis situations.

We must also stress the importance of *exercising the EOC itself* apart from any events that test the emergency response functions of firefighters, EMS, or other emergency personnel. The command, control, communication, and

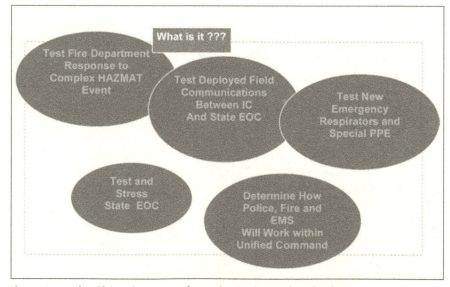

Figure 9.1   Identifying the Focus of Exercise Design and Evaluation.

coordination issues that an ordinary EOC must contend with are daunting and too often overlooked as automatic. They need to be consistently tested in TTXs and regular reviews of how an EOC can streamline and improve its operations. The functions, responsibilities, and tasks of the EOC should never be underestimated or taken for granted. Distinct activities that form the overall nucleus of emergency response takes place in an EOC and these activities must be understood and sharpened along with every other boilerplate element of emergency response. Moreover, I strongly feel that role reversals and switching of conventional emergency roles is very important for emergency responders to understand the functions, tasks, and demands of others. This means fire chiefs play in the EOC and EOC members deploy with fire companies. Police chiefs spend time in the EOC, and EOC staff roll out with police cruisers to grasp what officers must contend with in a normal exercise. Sometimes, the only way to grasp another's job is to perform that role in a "no-fault" exercise and the intricacies of another's function can be revealed.

We have discussed the vital role of scenario development and its linkage to validating EOPs, to test new equipment, to further train responders on novel emergency situations and to raise issues that have challenged emergency staff in the past. We understand that scenario development requires a mixture of realism, fiction, and complexity laden with enough ambiguity to fairly replicate real life.

Key Steps in Scenario Development

- Research the issue or problem
- Determine key components
- Develop a simple, yet credible, narrative
- Arrange flow of key events and context
- Balance specificity and ambiguity
- Vet the draft with experts
- Finalize the scenario

Testing actual relationships laterally between the local EOC and all deployed emergency response elements is essential, just as is the testing of routine cooperation and communication between local and state EOCs in complex emergencies. If this is not done, the coordinating activities and tasks related to effective emergency response may be lost or misunderstood. These aspects deserve regular exercising if possible.

We have discussed the importance of exercise organization in the design and scheduling of MSEL events and the sequencing of various activities closely coordinated with response cell and communications support staff in advance. It is amply clear that an exercise cannot be drafted on the back of a napkin and thrust into immediate action without careful thought and analysis of all the factors impinging on players. In fact, we can appreciate the degree of order that exercise organization requires us to consider.

Exercise Organization

- Setting, scope, and assumptions
- Designate STARTEX and ENDEX
- MSEL + scenario + scripted events
- Freeplay—injects—novel problems
- Exercise time—elapsed hours/days
- Daytime, weekend or 24/7 stress
- Stop action and hotwash
- Player feedback and evaluations

We have discussed the significance of finding skilled and objective evaluators who bring expertise and insight to the process. We understand the evaluation process entails many subdivisions of work in order to properly assess player performance. It is not enough to have the expected outcome outlined on the MSEL or for evaluators to review a checklist of desired performance. We know that evaluation takes time and skill and significant planning. It should be mentioned, that once the exercise is complete and the hotwash is conducted, it is useful to allow players some additional time to decompress from the event, especially if the activities were very intense or involved mass casualty situations that overwhelmed emergency responders. If by design the exercise was deliberately stressful to underscore the complexity of resolving the crisis, players may need time to reflect on events and relax.

We have stressed the importance of evaluators focusing on key aspects of their job and not losing sight of their overall purpose. There are many important tasks to complete in the evaluation process and they all play a significant role.

EVALUATION ISSUES

- Evaluation template
- Evaluator training
- ENDEX versus stop action
- Interviews versus observations
- Hotwash capture versus intensive follow-up
- Quicklook versus AAR
- Assessing controllers/directors and players
- Report writing and recommendations

Finally, we have tried to draw attention to those building blocks of effort and imagination that must be a part of every exercise. The steps suggested are meant to be general guidance rather than strict gospel requirements, However, the implication clearly is that your chances of success and effective results will increase dramatically if these basic steps and their associated injunctions are followed. There is always the risk in any exercise that things can go wrong and certain activities may not pan out as intended. *The key is to maintain professional regard for your staff and keep safety and security issues paramount in all your planning and pre-exercise work.* The proof of your efforts and the validation of your work will be better understood and appreciated when you have worn the "hat" of a controller, response cell staffer, evaluator, and player at least once in your life. One should never embark in any of those areas—especially exercise control and evaluation—without previous experience as a player and without due regard for all the work that has gone before you. Always take the opportunity to learn from others in the field how best to improve or strengthen your overall exercise design and evaluation projects drawing on LLIS (Lessons Learned Information Systems), academic papers, research studies, the experiences of other communities in exercises, and the significantly diverse resources of the Internet.

At this writing, recent news articles have noted the decline in interest at the DHS for the National Level Exercise 2011 to follow conventional terrorist scenarios, which has been the case largely since the infamous 9/11 attacks. This suggests that emphasis may shift more toward massive natural disaster scenarios and less toward terrorism. This could be a trend worth watching, as shifts in national emphasis may change and with it the available pass-through resources that state and local governments may use for their own exercise programs and the specific threat issues they examine.

This book's intention is to fill a serious gap in available academic literature and spell out the specific issues and fundamentals in emergency exercise design and evaluation. Hopefully, it has done that for you the reader in simple and unambiguous terms. It will prove valuable to me to know that both practicing emergency managers and students pursuing a graduate or undergraduate degree in emergency management found the book helpful and insightful. Enjoy the future—it brings hope, opportunity, and challenges.

Appendix A

Glossary

Readers should examine the array of publications available from FEMA and DHS on exercise design and research the HSEEP website for further information. Consider also "Select Emergency Management-Related Terms and Definitions" compiled by Wayne Blanchard, PhD, CEM, FEMA emergency management higher education project manager, for use in the Higher Education Project course Theory, Principles and Fundamentals of Hazards, Disasters and U.S. Emergency Management.

acceptable risk: That level of risk that is sufficiently low that society is comfortable with it. Risks will vary depending on the type of specific threat implied, where tornados and hurricanes may provide warning, while explosions and earthquakes may not. Communities accept levels of risk that roughly correspond to their preparedness to escape or shelter against the threat.

alert: Advisory that hazard is approaching but is less imminent than implied by warning message. Many Emergency Operations Plans provide for alerts to be delivered using different modes of communication depending on the emergency and the amount of time to provide ample warning so affected citizens and businesses can take shelter, evacuate, or consider other suitable protective actions.

assessment: Survey of a real or potential disaster to estimate the actual or expected damages and to make recommendations for prevention, preparedness, and response. The UN uses this term for post-emergency analysis of preliminary damages to buildings, key infrastructure, and populated areas. It can also be a survey of a real or potential disaster to estimate the actual or expected damages and to make recommendations for preparedness, mitigation, and relief action. In evaluation terms, it is an informed objective judgment about the performance and capability of a designated emergency response element.

After-Action Report: Formal review of exercise events with findings and recommendations for suggested corrective actions often written and delivered by evaluators after complete review of exercise notes, interviews, and observations. Typically the AAR is delivered to the client community leaders or senior emergency manager, along with an optional briefing, within thirty days after ENDEX.

briefing: Evaluators and controllers can deliver detailed presentations of a technical nature to prepare exercise staff for an exercise or brief senior political officials and visitors about the outcome of certain exercise events. Briefings can also be delivered to exercise players to prepare them for an exercise or when the AAR is completed and further insights about the exercise are needed.

catastrophe: Typically defined as an event leading to 500 deaths or $10 million in damages, but the overall effects, regardless of deaths, injuries, or estimated damages in dollars, are catastrophic according to the degree to which the affected area is capable of a rapid recovery versus situations where extensive and prolonged external assistance and intervention is required to enable a full recovery of the affected area. A catastrophe not only disrupts society, but also may cause a total breakdown in day-to-day functioning. One aspect of catastrophes is that most community functions disappear, there is no immediate leadership, hospitals may be damaged or destroyed, and the damage may be so great and so extensive that survivors have nowhere to turn for help.

catastrophic disaster: An event that results in large numbers of deaths and injuries; causes extensive damage or destruction of facilities that provide and sustain human needs; produces an overwhelming demand on state and local response resources and mechanisms; causes a severe long-term effect on general economic activity; and severely affects state, local, and private-sector capabilities to begin and sustain response activities. Note: the Stafford Act provides no definition for this term.

Category 1 hurricane: The lowest of five levels of relative hurricane intensity on the Saffir/Simpson hurricane scale. A Category 1 hurricane is defined by winds of 74–95 mph or a storm surge of four to five feet above normal. This category normally does not cause real damage to permanent structures, although damage to unanchored mobile homes, shrubbery, and trees can be expected. Also some coastal road flooding and minor pier damage. (Notification Manual)

Category 2 hurricane: The second of five levels of relative hurricane intensity on the Saffir/Simpson hurricane scale. A Category 2 hurricane is defined by winds of 96–110 mph, or a storm surge of six to eight feet above normal. This category normally causes some roofing material, door, and window damage to buildings. Considerable damage to vegetation, mobile homes, and piers can be expected. Coastal and low-lying escape routes can be expected to flood two to four hours before arrival of storm center. Small craft in unprotected anchorages will break mooring. (Notification Manual)

Category 3 hurricane: The third of five levels of relative hurricane intensity on the Saffir/Simpson hurricane scale. A Category 3 hurricane is defined by winds of 111–130 mph or a storm surge of nine to twelve feet above normal. This category normally does some structural damage to small residences and utility buildings, with a minor amount of curtain wall failures. Mobile homes are destroyed. Flooding near the coast can be expected to destroy smaller structures, with larger structures damaged by floating debris. Terrain continuously lower than five feet above sea level may be flooded inland as far as six miles. (Notification Manual)

Category 4 hurricane: The fourth of five levels of relative hurricane intensity on the Saffir/Simpson hurricane scale. A Category 4 hurricane is defined by winds of 131–155 mph or a storm surge of thirteen to eighteen feet above normal. This category normally causes more extensive curtain wall failures, with some complete roof structure failure on small residences. Major erosion will occur at beach areas. Major damage to lower floors of structures near the shore can be expected. Terrain continuously lower than ten feet above sea level may be flooded, requiring massive evacuation of residential areas inland as far as six miles. (Notification Manual)

Category 5 hurricane: The severest of five levels of relative hurricane intensity on the Saffir/Simpson hurricane scale. A Category 5 hurricane is defined by winds greater than 155 mph, or a storm surge greater than eighteen feet above normal. This category normally causes complete roof failure on many residential and industrial buildings; some are blown over or away. Major damage to lower floors of all structures located less than fifteen feet above sea level and within 500 yards of the shoreline can be expected. Massive evacuation of residential areas on low ground within five to ten miles of the shoreline may be required. (Notification Manual)

ChEmtREC: The Chemical Transportation Emergency Center, twenty-four-hour contact number 1-800-424-9300 in the continental United States, 202-483-7616 outside the continental United States. A service sponsored by the chemical industry that provides two stages of assistance to responders dealing with potentially hazardous materials. First, on receipt of a call providing the name of a chemical judged by the responder to be a potentially hazardous material, CHEMTREC provides immediate advice on the nature of the chemical product and the steps to be taken in handling it. Second, CHEMTREC promptly contacts the shipper of the material involved for more detailed information and on-scene assistance when feasible. (DOT 1993)

civil disturbances: Group acts of violence and disorders prejudicial to public law and order within the fifty states, District of Columbia, Commonwealth of Puerto Rico, U.S. possessions and territories, or any political subdivision thereof. As more specifically defined in DoD Directive 3025.12 (Military Support to Civil Authorities), "civil disturbance" includes all domestic conditions requiring the use of federal armed forces. (Title 32 CFR 185)

civil emergency: Any natural or man-made disaster or emergency that causes or could cause substantial harm to the population or infrastructure. This term can include a "major disaster" or "emergency" as those terms are defined in the Stafford Act, as amended, as well as consequences of an attack or a national security emergency. Under 42 U.S.C. 5121, the terms "major disaster" and "emergency" are defined substantially by action of the president in declaring that extant circumstances and risks justify his implementation of the legal powers provided by those statutes. (Title 32 CFR 185)

comprehensive emergency management: CEM refers to a state's responsibility and unique capability to manage all types of disasters by coordinating wide-ranging actions of numerous agencies. The "comprehensive" aspect of CEM includes all four phases of disaster activity: mitigation, preparedness, response, and recovery for all risks—attack, man-made, and natural—in a federal-state-local operating partnership.

Comprehensive Environmental Response, Compensation and Liability Act (CERCLA): Public Law 96-510, as amended. More popularly known as "Superfund," CERCLA provides authority for federal and state governments to respond directly to hazardous substances incidents. (FEMA 1992, Appendix C)

consequence management (Com): Involves measures to alleviate the damage, loss, hardship, or suffering caused by emergencies. It includes measures to restore essential government services, protect public health and safety, and provide emergency relief to affected governments, businesses, and individuals, especially when resulting from a catastrophic emergency with significant damage caused by weapons of mass destruction, nuclear accident, or pandemic.

contingency planning: Tactical and practical measures designed to enable a high rate of survival in a disaster or crisis situation through prudent preplanning, storage of essentials, and strategies for emerging from the disaster intact.

continuity of government: All measures that may be taken to ensure the continuity of essential functions of governments in the event of emergency conditions, including line-of-succession for key decision-makers.

crisis: Crises involve events and processes that carry severe threat, uncertainty, an unknown outcome, and urgency typically caused by natural forces, technological systems failures, or hazmat accidents where toxic or dangerous substances pose threats to nearby populations. Most crises have trigger points so critical as to leave historical marks on nations, groups, and individual lives. Some are readily resolved and some can only be alleviated. Crises are historical points of reference, distinguishing between the past and the present. They come in a variety of forms, such as terrorism, natural disasters, nuclear plant accidents, and pandemics requiring intervention and oversight by the national government to restore order, civil calm, and public safety

crisis management: Crisis management can mean either the management of a crisis after it has arisen or it can mean intervening in a near-crisis situation or managing in such a way that a crisis does not arise in the first place. Often this is seen as how one responds to an existent crisis or how one might anticipate crises and therefore be able to respond to them. Crisis management most often connotes crisis intervention management, whether after the onset of the disaster or in anticipation of a disaster. Key to crisis management is an accurate and timely diagnosis of the criticality of the problems and the dynamics of events that ensue. Knowledge, skills, courageous leadership full of risk-taking ability, and vigilance are often the hallmarks of effective crisis management. Successful crisis management also requires motivation, a sense of urgency, commitment, and creative thinking with a long-term strategic vision. Successful crisis management requires: (1) sensing the urgency of the matter, (2) thinking creatively and strategically to solving the crisis, (3) taking bold actions and acting courageously and sincerely, (4) breaking away from the self-protective organizational culture by taking risks and actions that may produce optimum solutions in which there would be no significant losers, and (5) maintaining a continuous presence in the rapidly changing situation with unfolding dramatic events.

damage assessment: The process utilized to determine the magnitude of damage and the unmet needs of individuals, businesses, the public sector, and the community caused by a disaster or emergency event. Usually performed within six hours after the initial disaster and then every day thereafter to assess where further remedial actions may be needed.

damage classification: Evaluation and recording of damage to structures, facilities, or objects according to three (or more) categories:

1. "Severe damage"—which precludes further use of the structure, facility, or object for its intended purpose.
2. "Moderate damage"—or the degree of damage to principal members, which precludes effective use of the structure, facility, or object for

its intended purpose, unless major repairs are made short of complete reconstruction.

3. "Light damage"—such as broken windows, slight damage to roofing and siding, interior partitions blown down, and cracked walls; the damage is not severe enough to preclude use of the installation for the purpose for which it was intended. (U.N. 1992, 19)

declaration: The formal action by the president to make a state eligible for major disaster or emergency assistance under the Robert T. Stafford Relief and Emergency Assistance Act, Public Law 93-288, as amended.

Defense Emergency Response fund: Established by Public Law 101-165 (1989). That law provides that, "The Fund shall be available for providing reimbursement to currently applicable appropriations of the Department of Defense for supplies and services provided in anticipation of requests from other Federal departments and agencies and from State and local governments for assistance on a reimbursable basis to respond to natural or manmade disasters. The Fund may be used upon a determination by the Secretary of Defense that immediate action is necessary before a formal request for assistance on a reimbursable basis is received." The Fund is applicable to military support to civil authorities (MSCA) under DoD Directive 3025.1 and to foreign disaster assistance under DoD Directive 5100.46. (32 CFR 185)

disaster: The distinction between natural hazards or disasters and their man-made (or technological) counterparts is often difficult to establish. Yet significant, widespread, and substantial damage is usually sustained by businesses, homes, people, and infrastructural systems that can often trigger additional environmental damage. Losses of life, property, and public safety and stability are profound and long lasting, requiring a sustained commitment to rebuilding and recovery. There is also the implication that disasters can be mitigated or prevented, which falls within our domain of responsibility, causing the reciprocal belief that society has a consequent obligation to attempt to prevent disasters. Disasters typically reveal areas of persistent vulnerability and societal weakness and can impose significant and strategic damage on centers of commerce, government, and society. Disasters may be local, regional, or national in scope, and may require levels of government intervention and assistance ranging from minimal to extensive. Thus government, citizens, and businesses must jointly prepare for them.

disaster management: Disaster management is the process of forming common objectives and common values in order to encourage participants to plan for and deal with potential and actual disasters. It is a complex process that assists communities to respond, both pre and post-disaster, in such a way as to save lives; preserve property; and maintain the ecological, economic, and political stability of the impacted region.

disaster, natural: Any hurricane, tornado, storm, flood, high water, wind-driven water, tidal wave, tsunami, earthquake, volcanic eruption, landslide, mudslide, snowstorm, drought, fire, or other catastrophe in any part of the United States that causes, or that may cause, substantial damage or injury to civilian property or persons. (Robert T. Stafford Act, 602)

disaster response: The collective and combined efforts of government, citizens, and the private sector to coordinate and assemble necessary resources to repair disaster damages and lay the foundation for eventual recovery of the affected area. A sum of decisions and actions taken during and after disaster, including immediate relief, rehabilitation, and reconstruction.

disaster, technological: Often refers to colossal systems failures of energy, telecommunications, nuclear power, and related infrastructural operations, where the failure either imposes a sustained risk on the immediate population and economy or contains the risk of secondary explosion, toxic exposure or equivalent harm to an adjacent community. Risks vary depending on the systems involved and may be contained and controlled or may overwhelm control mechanisms and cause harmful long-term effects to the surrounding area despite interventions to manage the accident or disaster.

domestic emergency: "Any natural disaster or other emergency that does not seriously endanger national security, but which is of such a catastrophic nature that it cannot be managed effectively without substantial Federal presence, or which arises within spheres of activity in which there is an established Federal role." (FEMA Disaster Dictionary 2001, 36; cites Domestic Emergencies Handbook, U.S. Army Forces Command, March 15, 1999).

Domestic Emergency support team (DEst): "Relative to terrorism incident operations, an organization formed by the Federal Bureau of Investigation (FBI) to provide expert advice and assistance to the FBI On-Scene Commander (OSC) related to the capabilities of the DEST agencies and to coordinate follow-on response assets. When deployed, the DEST merges into the existing Joint Operations Center (JOC) structure." (FEMA Disaster Dictionary 2001, 36; cites FEMA FRP).

emergency: An unexpected event that places life and/or property in danger and requires an immediate response through the use of routine community resources and procedures. Examples would be a multi-automobile wreck, especially involving injury or death, and a fire caused by lightning strike that spreads to other buildings. Any hurricane, tornado, storm, flood, high water, wind-driven water, tidal wave, tsunami, earthquake, volcanic eruption, landslide, mudslide, snowstorm, drought, fire, explosion, nuclear accident, or other natural or man-made catastrophe in any part of the

United States. Any occasion or instance for which, in the determination of the president, federal assistance is needed to supplement state and local efforts and capabilities to save lives and to protect property and public health and safety or to lessen the threat of a catastrophe in any part of the United States. (FEMA 1990)

emergency (Stafford Act): "Any occasion or instance for which, in the determination of the President, Federal assistance is needed to supplement State and local efforts to save lives and to protect property and public health and safety, or to lessen or avert the threat of a catastrophe in any part of the United States. The Governor of a State, or the Acting Governor in his/her absence, may request that the President declare an emergency when an incident occurs or threatens to occur in a State which would not qualify under the definition of a major disaster. Assistance authorized by an emergency declaration is limited to immediate and short-term assistance, and may not exceed $5 million, except when authorized by the FEMA Associate Director for Response and Recovery under certain conditions." (FEMA Disaster Dictionary 2001, 39; cites Robert T. Stafford Act 102; 44 CFR 206.2, 206.35; 206.63, 206.66, and 503)

emergency assistance: Assistance that may be made available under an emergency declaration. In general, federal support to state and local efforts to save lives, protect property and public health and safety, and lessen or avert the threat of a catastrophe. Federal emergency assistance may take the form of coordinating all disaster relief assistance (including voluntary assistance) provided by federal agencies, private organizations, and state and local governments. Or, the federal government may provide technical and advisory assistance to affected state and local governments for: the performance of essential community services; issuance of warnings of risks or hazards; public health and safety information, including dissemination of such information; provision of health and safety measures; management, control, and reduction of immediate threats to public health and safety; debris removal; temporary housing; and distribution of medicine, food, and other consumable supplies. (Stafford Act)

emergency management: The entire process of planning and intervention for rescue and relief to reduce the impact of emergencies as well as the response and recovery measures to mitigate the significant social, economic, and environmental consequences to communities and ultimately to the country, usually through an emergency operation center (EOC). The process by which the uncertainties that exist in potentially hazardous situations can be minimized and public safety maximized. The goal is to limit the costs of emergencies or disasters through the implementation of a series of strategies and tactics reflecting the full life cycle of disaster (i.e., preparedness, response, recovery, and mitigation). Emergency management is the discipline and profession of applying science, technology, planning, and management to deal with extreme events that can injure or kill large numbers of people, do extensive damage to property, and disrupt community life. It involves organized analysis, planning, decision making, and assignment of available resources to mitigate (lessen the effect of or prevent) prepare for, respond to, and recover from the effects of all hazards. The goal of emergency management is to save lives, prevent injuries, and protect property and the environment if an emergency occurs.

emergency manager: The person who has the day-to-day responsibility for emergency management programs and activities for a village, community, township, city, county, or state. The role is one of coordinating all aspects of a jurisdiction's mitigation, preparedness, response, and recovery capabilities. They are professionals who practice the discipline of emergency management by applying science, technology, planning, and management techniques to coordinate the activities of a wide array of agencies and organizations dedicated to preventing and responding to extreme events that threaten, disrupt, or destroy lives or property.

Emergency Operations Plan (EOP): An all-hazards document that specifies actions to be taken in the event of an emergency or disaster event; identifies authorities, relationships, and the actions to be taken by whom, what, when, and where, based on predetermined assumptions, objectives, and existing capabilities.

emergency preparedness: Activities and measures designed or undertaken to prepare for or minimize the effects of a hazard upon the civilian population, to deal with the immediate emergency conditions that would be created by the hazard, and to effectuate emergency repairs to, or the emergency restoration of, vital utilities and facilities destroyed or damaged by the hazard. (Stafford Act)

emergency public information: Information that is disseminated primarily in anticipation of an emergency or at the actual time of an emergency and in addition to providing information as such, frequently directs actions, instructs, and transmits direct orders. (Simeon Institute 1998)

emergency risk management: "Emergency risk management is a 'systematic process that produces a range of measures that contribute to the well-being of communities and the environment.' It includes: context definition; risk identification; risk analysis; risk evaluation; risk treatment; monitoring and reviewing; and, communicating and consulting." (Emergency Management Australia 2000, 1)

emergency support services: The departments of local government that have the capability to respond to emergencies twenty-four hours a day. They typically include law enforcement, fire, rescue, and public works.

They may also be referred to as emergency response personnel or emergency operating forces.

federal radiological emergency response plan (FRERP): The plan used by federal agencies to respond to a radiological emergency, with or without a Stafford Act declaration. Without a Stafford Act declaration, federal agencies respond to radiological emergencies using the FRERP, each agency in accordance with existing statutory authorities and funding resources. The lead federal agency has responsibility for coordination of the overall federal response to the emergency. FEMA is responsible for coordinating non-radiological support using the structure of the Federal Response Plan. When a major disaster or emergency is declared under the Stafford Act and an associated radiological emergency exists, the functions and responsibilities of the FRERP remain the same. The lead federal agency coordinates the management of the radiological response with the Federal Coordinating Officer. Although the direction of the radiological response remains the same with the lead federal agency, the FCO has the overall responsibility for coordination of federal assistance in support of state and local governments using the FRERP.

four phases: Mitigation, preparedness, response, and recovery. These phases refer to distinct areas of effort related to emergency management. Resilience is often added as a fifth element to reflect a commitment to sustained strategic recovery and rapid restoration of essential services.

hazard: Hazards are natural, technological, or social phenomena that pose a threat to people and their surroundings, often resulting from interaction of physical and human systems. They can include dangerous natural or man-made phenomena that expose a vulnerable location to disastrous events. Vulnerability reduction aims at neutralizing the dangers posed by the hazard. The hazard is the potential, the disaster is the actual event. A hazard is a natural or man-made phenomenon that may cause physical damage, economic losses, or threaten human life and well-being if it occurs in an area of human settlement, agricultural, or industrial activity. Hazards are part of our natural environment and steps should be taken to prepare contingency plans for situations where hazards will affect populated areas, interfere with commerce, or disrupt government.

hazard analysis: The identification and evaluation of all hazards that potentially threaten a jurisdiction to determine the degree of threat that is posed by each. That part of the overall planning process that identifies and describes hazards and their effects upon the community. Hazard assessment involves analysis of formal and informal historical records, and skilled interpretation of existing topographical, geological, geomorphological, hydrological, and land-use maps.

hazard, environmental: "Events which directly threaten human life and property by means of acute physical or chemical trauma. ... Any manageable definition of environmental hazards will be both arbitrary and contentious." But, despite their diverse sources, most disasters have a number of common features:

1. The origin of the damaging process or event is clear and produces characteristic threats to human life or well-being, for example a flood causes death by drowning.
2. The warning time is normally short, that is the hazards are often known as rapid-onset events. This means that they can be unexpected even though they occur within a known hazard zone, such as the floodplain of a small river basin.
3. Most of the direct losses, whether to life or property, are suffered fairly shortly after the event, i.e., within days or weeks.
4. The exposure to hazard, or assumed risk, is largely involuntary, normally due to the location of people in a hazardous area (e.g., the unplanned expansion of some Third World cities onto unstable hillslopes).
5. The resulting disaster occurs with an intensity that justifies an emergency response, that is the provision of specialist aid to the victims. The scale of response can vary from local to international."

hazard, technological: Typically man-related hazards such as nuclear power plant accidents, industrial plant explosions, aircraft crashes, dam breaks, mine cave-ins, pipeline explosions, and hazardous material accidents. A range of hazards emanating from the manufacture, transportation, and use of such substances as radioactive materials, chemicals, explosives, flammables, agricultural pesticides, herbicides, and disease agents; oil spills on land, coastal waters, or inland water systems; and debris from space. (FEMA 1992, FRP Appendix B) Technological hazards are best seen as accidental failures of design or management affecting large-scale structures, transport systems, or industrial activities that present life-threatening risks to the local community; the failure "trigger" that provokes a technological disaster is likely to arise for one of the following reasons: (1) defective design, (2) inadequate management, (3) sabotage or terrorism (Smith 1996, 316).

hazardous material (hazmat): Any material that is explosive, flammable, poisonous, corrosive, reactive, or radioactive (or any combination), and requires special care in handling because of the hazards posed to public health, safety, and/or the environment. Hazmat situations and emergencies can lead to widespread disasters if left unmanaged and include all manner of technological and environmental hazards ranging from localized systems failures to catastrophic explosions and toxic releases of material. Special hazmat emergency response units with modern specialized equipment, technology, and training are often required to manage hazmat emergencies.

incident: "Any condition that meets the definition of major disaster or emergency which causes damage or hardship that may result in a Presidential declaration of a major disaster or an emergency." (FEMA Disaster Dictionary 2001, 62–63, citing Title 44 CFR 206.32) "Under the ICS concept, an incident is an occurrence, either human-caused or by natural phenomena, that requires action by emergency service personnel to prevent or minimize loss of life or damage to property and/or natural resources." (FEMA Disaster Dictionary 2001, 62–63, citing National Wildfire Coordinating Group, Incident Command System, National Training Curriculum, ICS Glossary (PMS 202, NFES #2432), October 1994)

incident command system (ICS): The combination of facilities, equipment, personnel, procedures, and communications operating within a common organizational structure with responsibility for management of assigned resources to effectively direct and control the response to an incident. It is intended to expand as the situation requires greater resources without requiring new, reorganized, command structures. See also DHS and FEMA guidance on this topic contained in Homeland Security Directives and FEMA instructions. A standardized on-scene emergency management concept specifically designed to allow its users to adopt an integrated organizational structure equal to the complexity and demands of single or multiple incidents, without being hindered by jurisdictional boundaries.

incident commander (IC): ICS term for the person, usually from the local jurisdiction, who is responsible for overall management of an incident. On most incidents, the command activity is carried out by a single IC. The IC may be assisted by a deputy from the same agency or from an assisting agency. (FEMA 1993)

inject: In exercise design this term typically refers to events and requirements crafted by response cell staff either in response to player actions or to stimulate further player actions intended to add complexity, realism, new details, new problems, new issues, or different perspectives into an exercise. Injects will be included in MSEL documents or agreed to in advance between controllers and response cell staff.

major disaster: Any natural catastrophe (including any hurricane, tornado, storm, high water, wind-driven water, tidal wave, tsunami, earthquake, volcanic eruption, landslide, mudslide, snowstorm, or drought) or, regardless of cause, any fire, flood, or explosion, in any part of the United States that, in the determination of the president, causes damage of sufficient severity and magnitude to warrant major disaster assistance under the Stafford Act to supplement the efforts and available resources of states, local governments, and disaster relief organizations in alleviating the damage, loss, hardship, or suffering caused thereby. (Robert T. Stafford Act 102; 44 CFR 206.2 and 206.36)

military support to civil authorities (MSCA): Those activities and measures taken by Department of Defense components to foster mutual assistance and support between DoD and any civil government agency in planning or preparedness for, or in the application of resources for response to, the consequences of civil emergencies or attacks, including national security emergencies. MSCA is described in DoD Directive 3025.1. The secretary of the Army is designated as the DoD executive agent for MSCA. (Title 32 CFR 185)

mitigate: To lessen in force or intensity. Mitigation is the deliberate governmental and social attempt to reduce the occurrence of a disaster, to reduce the vulnerability of certain populations, and to more equitably distribute the costs within the society. It includes those activities designed to alleviate the effects of a major disaster or emergency or long-term activities to minimize the potentially adverse effects of future disaster in affected areas. It also means taking all steps necessary to minimize the potentially adverse effects of the proposed action and to restore, preserve, and enhance natural values of wetlands; or long-term activities to minimize the potentially adverse effects of future disaster in affected areas·

Master Scenario Events List (MSEL): This document is compiled by exercise designers, controllers, and support staff to identify the entire schedule, sequence of events and taskers, and key exercise messages, and to designate time-linked expected outcomes for every aspect of the emergency exercise. It specifies STARTEX, ENDEX, and all activities in between including instances where interventions or stop-action may be authorized by controllers. Highly detailed and arranged by sequential release of exercise events, the MSEL summarizes all significant exercise activity to be played during the exercise.

national disaster medical system (NDMS): A federally coordinated initiative to augment the nation's emergency medical response capability by providing medical assets to be used during major disasters or emergencies. NDMS has three major components: Disaster Medical Assistance Teams and Clearing-Staging Units to provide triage, patient stabilization, and austere medical services at a disaster site; an evacuation capability for movement of patients from a disaster area to locations where definitive medical care can be provided; and a voluntary hospital network to provide definitive medical care. NDMS is administered by the Department of Health and Human Services/U.S. Public Health Service, in cooperation with the Department of Defense, the Department of Veterans Affairs, FEMA, state and local governments, and the private sector. (Facts on the NDMS)

national security emergency: "Any occurrence, including natural disaster, military attack, technological emergency, or other emergency, that seriously degrades or seriously threatens the national security of the United States." (FEMA Disaster Dictionary 2001, 84; cites Executive Order 12656—Also see NSPD and HSPD documents that deal with this topic)

plume: Identifiable stream of air with a temperature or composition different from that of its environment. Examples are a smoke plume from a chimney and a buoyant plume rising by convection from heated ground. Plumes associated with toxic, pathogenic, or radiological releases of harmful material must be traced and estimates of their direction, speed, and dynamics must be plotted.

preliminary damage assessment (PDA): A process used to determine the impact and magnitude of damage and the resulting unmet needs of individuals, businesses, the public sector, and the community as a whole. Information collected as a result of the PDA process is used by the state as a basis for the governor's request for federal assistance under the Stafford Act, and by FEMA to document the recommendation made to the president in response to the governor's request. (44 CFR 206.33)

preparedness: Those activities, programs, and systems that exist prior to an emergency that are used to support and enhance response to an emergency or disaster. Establishing and delineating authorities and responsibilities for emergency actions and making provisions for having the people, equipment, and facilities in place to respond when the need arises. Preparedness involves planning, training, exercising, procuring, and maintaining equipment, and designating facilities for shelters and other emergency purposes. It also involves the development and regular testing of warning systems (linked to forecasting systems) and plans for evacuation or other measures to be taken during a disaster alert period to minimize potential loss of life and physical damage; the education and training of officials and the population at risk; the establishment of policies, standards, organizational arrangements, and operational plans to be applied following a disaster impact; the securing of resources (possibly including the stockpiling of supplies and the earmarking of funds); and the training of intervention teams. More specifically, it includes the entire collection of procedures, routines, training, and activities that emergency response staff take in preparing them for an actual emergency. These measures are completed well in advance of any emergency to ensure effective response to the impact of disasters, including the issuance of timely and effective early warnings, assembly of critical technologies, and the temporary removal of people and property from a threatened location. In exercise terms, this encompasses all responder behavior before an actual emergency situation occurs to account for player preparedness.

prevention: Encompasses activities designed to provide permanent protection from disasters. It includes engineering and other physical protective measures, and also legislative measures controlling land use and urban planning. This includes all activities to provide outright avoidance of the adverse impact of hazards and related environmental, technological, and natural disasters.

radiological emergency: A radiological incident that poses an actual, potential, or perceived hazard to public health or safety or loss of property. (FRERP, Appendix B)

recovery: A coordinated process of supporting emergency-affected communities in reconstruction of the physical infrastructure and restoration of emotional, social, economic, and physical well-being immediately following a disaster. Those long-term activities and programs beyond the initial crisis period of an emergency or disaster and designed to return all systems to normal status or to reconstitute these systems to a new condition that is less vulnerable.

resilience: The capacity to recover successfully from loss and damage caused by disasters in a rapid and comprehensive manner as a result of deliberate pre-crisis planning jointly by citizens, businesses, academia, and government. Beyond the recovery level it is a robust and thriving enterprise that was deliberately engineered before the crisis to emerge rapidly and repair all damaged infrastructures, commercial sites, neighborhoods, and governmental operations. It has personal, familial, organizational, societal, and governmental dimensions featuring a community's capability of organizing itself, increasing its capacity for learning, and promoting adaptation in recovery from a disaster.

response: Those activities and programs designed to address the immediate and short-term effects of the onset of an emergency or disaster. (FEMA 1992) Activities to address the immediate and short-term effects of an emergency or disaster. Response includes immediate actions to save lives, protect property, and meet basic human needs. Based on the requirements of the situation, response assistance will be provided to an affected state under the Federal Response Plan using a partial activation of selected emergency support functions (ESFs) or the full activation of all twelve ESFs to meet the needs of the situation. (FEMA FRP, Appendix B)

risk: A measure of the probability of damage to life, property, and/or the environment that could occur if a hazard manifests itself, including the anticipated severity of consequences to people. It is the product of hazard and vulnerability (V) as they affect a series of elements (E) comprising the population, properties, economic activities, public services, and so on, under the threat of disaster in a given area. Risk is estimated by combining the probability of events and the consequences (usually conceptualized as losses) that would arise if the events take place.

risk analysis: Process that involves identifying, measuring, or estimating and evaluating risk. A detailed examination performed to understand the nature of unwanted, negative consequences to human life, health, property, or the environment; an analytical process to provide information regarding undesirable events; the process of quantification of the probabilities and expected consequences for identified risks. It incorporates estimates of the probability of various levels of injury and damage to provide a more complete description of the risk from the full range of possible hazard events in the area.

risk management: Public risk management is a process that is used to decide what to do where a risk has been determined to exist. It involves identifying the level of tolerance the community has for a specific risk or set of risks and determines what risk assessment options are acceptable within a social, economic, cultural, and political context. To achieve this, the process must be open since it has to factor in benefits, costs of control, and any statutory or socially approved requirements needed to manage the risk. The process of intervening to reduce risk—the making of public and private decisions regarding protective policies and actions that reduce the threat to life, property, and the environment posed by hazards. Generally, the risk management process attempts to answer the following questions: (1) What can be done? (2) What options or alternatives are available and what are their associated trade-offs in terms of costs, benefits, and other current and future risks? (3) What are the effects of current decisions on future options?

risk reduction: Long-term measures to reduce the scale and/or the duration of eventual adverse effects of unavoidable or unpreventable disaster hazards on a society that is at risk, by reducing the vulnerability of its people, structures, services, and economic activities to the impact of known disaster hazards. Typical risk reduction measures include improved building standards, floodplain zoning and land-use planning, crop diversification, and planting windbreaks.

Stafford Act: The Robert T. Stafford Disaster Relief and Emergency Assistance Act, Public Law 93-288, as amended. The Stafford Act provides an orderly and continuing means of assistance by the federal government to state and local governments in carrying out their responsibilities to alleviate the suffering and damage that result from disaster. The president, in response to a state governor's request, may declare an "emergency" or "major disaster" in order to provide federal assistance under the act. The president, in Executive Order 12148, delegated all functions, except those in Sections 301, 401, and 409, to the Director, of FEMA. The act provides for the appointment of a federal coordinating officer who will operate in the designated area with a state coordinating officer for the purpose of coordinating state and local disaster assistance efforts with those of the federal government. (44 CFR 206.2)

tasker: Identifies a specific exercise assignment or activity that ordinarily includes a launching time, a request for player action, and expected outcomes as described in the MSEL document. When assigned to players during the course of an exercise, taskers can be inserted via phone, fax, e-mail, written letter, TV announcement, or other suitable vehicle for communicating the issue or problem that the tasker frames as a problem for exercise players to solve.

terrorism: "The calculated use of unlawful violence or threat of unlawful violence to inculcate fear; intended to coerce or to intimidate governments or societies in the pursuit of goals that are generally political, religious, or ideological." (FEMA Disaster Dictionary 2001, 120; citing DoD Joint Pub 1-102)

unified Command: "Under the ICS (Incident Command System) concept of operations, Unified Command is a unified team effort which allows all agencies with responsibility for an incident, either geographical or functional, to manage an incident by establishing a common set of incident objectives and strategies. This Unified Command effort is accomplished without losing or abdicating agency authority, responsibility, or accountability." (FEMA Disaster Dictionary 2001, 124; citing ICS Glossary)

vulnerability: The extent to which infrastructures, commercial and industrial operations, homes, businesses, and government operations are subject to disruption, damage, and loss as a result of natural disasters, hazards, or technological-environmental disasters. The degree of weakness and overall susceptibility to damage and losses as well as the negative impacts of a disaster owing to a lack of protective measures or mitigation and riskreduction actions.

vulnerability analysis: Identifies what is susceptible to damage. Should provide information on extent of the vulnerable zone; population, in terms of size and types that could be expected to be within the vulnerable zone; private and public property that may be damaged, including essential support systems and transportation corridors; and environments that may be affected. The process of estimating the vulnerability to potential disaster hazards of specified elements at risk. It involves consideration of all significant elements in society, including physical, social, and economic considerations (both short and long term), and the extent to which essential services (and traditional and local coping mechanisms) are able to continue functioning. Often, the analysis consists of these steps: (1) identify potential threats to the system, (2) verify that the vulnerability of the system is acceptable, (3) verify that the system's security actions and installations, and safety functions are adequate, (4) evaluate the cost-effectiveness of a proposed action to reduce its inherent vulnerability

vulnerability assessment: Evaluation of the likely degree of loss to a risk or a set of hazards. It characterizes the exposed populations and property and the extent of injury and damage that may result from a natural hazard event of a given intensity in a given area. It combines the information from the hazard identification with an inventory of the existing (or planned) property and population exposed to a hazard. It provides information on who and what are vulnerable to a natural hazard within the geographic areas defined by hazard identification. Vulnerability assessment can also estimate damage and casualties that will result from various intensities of the hazard. This would necessarily include estimates of the number of people exposed to hazards (including special populations such as the elderly, hospitalized, disabled, and concentrated populations such as children in schools); the property exposed; and the critical facilities exposed (such as medical care facilities, bridges, sewage treatment and water pumping and treatment plants, power plants, and police and fire stations).

warning: Dissemination of message signaling imminent hazard that may include advice on protective measures. A warning is issued by the National Weather Service to let people know that a severe weather event is already occurring or is imminent. People should take immediate safety action. It is an emergency advisory issued by competent government authority.

NOTE: Students, exercise designers and emergency management leaders are urged to chck the DHS and FEMA websites for further details on how to enlarge and modify this brief glossary and add valuable definitions and operational terms of value and significance to the lexicon of improved emergency management.

Appendix B

Evaluation Guides

Exercise Evaluation Guides (EEGs) have been developed as tools to assist the evaluation of the performance of the tasks, activities, and capabilities necessary to prevent, protect against, respond to, and recover from natural and man-made disasters. EEGs do not have to be developed for every exercise, but they will help enormously in simplifying the array of tasks and activities to be evaluated and provide some level of organizational detail to assist evaluators in making sound judgments about what really happened during the exercise.

An EEG is very different a MSEL although the connection between the two activities is important. While the MSEL carefully scripts and outlines all exercise activities the EEG provides a tracking mechanism to draw attention to key behaviors, tasks and activities that should receive scrutiny by evaluators. EEGs help confirm that key MSEL events were the subject of exercise activity and merit special review to determine not only if taskers, incidents and problems were dealt with by exercise players but also how well, how rapidly, how effectively and how smoothly.

The EEGs are foundational to exercise evaluation, improvement plans, and corrective actions. They are documents that assist with the exercise evaluation process by providing evaluators with consistent standards and guidelines for observation, data collection, analysis, and report writing. This tracks with major events itemized in the MSEL. Examples of how the EEG can be constructed to assist evaluators is illustrated in the table below.

Table B.1   Emergency Management Activities of the EOC

Task	Outcome	Response Element
31 Issued 10:19 day 1	Alert and mobilize EOC staff	EOC staff
32 Issued 10:21 day 1	Activate and expand EOC	EOC Staff
33 Issued 10:27 day 1	Direct and control response operations	EOC staff
34 Issued 10:35 day 1	Notify government agencies and officials—alert state EOC	EOC staff
35 Issued 10:39 day 1	Issue public alert and warning via approved mechanisms	EOC staff
36 Issued 10:41 day 1	Transfer warning messages to special needs and non-English-language populations	EOC staff
37 Issued 10:45 day 1		

Appendix C

MSEL Sample

Actions required by MSEL events are caused by an implementing message that is designed to prompt play or response. The document that causes all or part of the action or activity is called an implementer. MSEL implementers are prepared for each MSEL event, regardless of the means of communication.

Complex exercises, as well as more fundamental exercises, should have a table of sequential MSELs in the ExPlan which track with a series of time sensitive tasks, requirements and nuggets of information intended to move the exercise forward. In many exercises the rate of MSELs is often paced at one MSEL every twenty minutes. Typical MSEL elements include a matrix based chart which reflects and summarizes these important elements:

- Inject message or theme (often a task, new information or requirement)
- Inject time
- Specify incoming source and recipient office
- Notes for evaluators on what specific actions should be observed
- A column which allows notes on what exercise players actually did

It contains all the pertinent information to be used for management control and tracking as well as controller instructions and the implementer information. It also contains the information the controller will use to inject the event into play. This data will be used in exercise evaluation. On the following page a sample MSEL item is described for reference.

Table C.1   Sample MSEL Implementer Form

Control and Evaluation Eyes Only			
Event Number	*Inject Time*	*From*	*To*
404	09/1620	ARC SW MS Chapter	ARC SHW Jackson, MS
Responsible Controller ARC	**Inject Means** Telephone	**Related Event(s)** 400, 401	**Objective Reference #s** ESF06-3.6
Points of Review	To be added by controller and evaluator		
Event Description	Request from local ARC Chapter for transportation and other support for a community college evacuation involving 42 handicapped students.		
Expected Action	State ARC Hurricane Watch advises the chapter that ARC cannot provide transportation directly, but the chapter must coordinate this through the County EMA EOC, in that this is the responsibility of both the college and local emergency management. Refers the chapter to the county EOC. If this is a problem, ARC Watch will inform the state ARC representative in the state EOC. Watch asks what other support is needed.		
Controller Note	This message would have originated from the college provost direct to the local ARC chapter or EOC as requested. That part is simulated.		

Appendix D

Tackling Tabletop Exercises
Looking at the Fundamental Issues

FUNDAMENTALS

Tabletops are designed to test functional operations, delivery of key emergency services, quality and timeliness of response, and performance of specified equipment or special technologies in a condensed and controlled environment. Often they are "no-fault" events that simply strive to underscore the essential tasks, duties, and major functional requirements levied on municipal and state emergency services staff.

Tabletops often are scheduled to run for two days or less with ample time for setup, observation, discussion, stop-action, expert lectures, and other techniques to focus on particular functions like public affairs, emergency alerts, damage assessments, and the operational aspects of the EOC. Often they are the cheapest and best way to align training and performance expectations so measures of actual capability and readiness can be determined.

KEY ELEMENTS

Tabletops begin with a scenario of usually one page summarizing the emergency incident and specifying through direct questions and inference the tasks and activities that are expected of emergency personnel. Sometimes the task is clear, and at other times deliberate ambiguity is included to determine how people will actually solve unexpected problems or emergencies where no guidance exists.

The next issue is to determine what specific response tasks you want to test or measure. Tabletops must lead players to perform these activities in a manner that replicates real life. Therefore, placing real people with their genuine functions into situations is best, but there are considerable virtues

187

derived from forcing players to adopt new roles and grasp what the issues, priorities, problems, and needs are in ways that ordinary lectures and reading cannot supply. Roles such as fire chief, hospital director, emergency manager, mayor, media reporter and many others add realism and place unique and valuable "real-world" demands on the players.

This requires that experts running the exercise, observers and evaluators reviewing team and individual performance, and those playing or just observing as trainees remain mindful of their roles while playing the tabletop. Often nothing is more important in conducting a tabletop than ensuring that all the players are afforded an opportunity to fulfill a task, perform a role or solve a problem. In this venue there is logic in verifying that a kind of functional coherence is at work enabling players to enact their assigned duties just as a real emergency would require. If players are allowed to be passive and avoid active participation the tabletop would be much less effective and valuable to the organization sponsoring it.

Finally it is crucial to capture feedback and commentary from players at the end of exercises and allow sufficient time for people to reflect and discuss what they saw and experienced. Those perspectives, along with the insights and comments collected by expert evaluators, provide valuable information that can allow improvements in training, group performance, skills development, and greater understanding of both the simple and complex issues involved in handling emergency events and trying to manage crises.

FUNCTIONAL DOMAINS TO BE TESTED AND EVALUATED IN A TABLETOP EXERCISE

1. Alert notification
   - To demonstrate the ability to alert, mobilize, and activate the personnel, facilities, and systems required for emergence response, and provide for subsequent shift change staffing to maintain twenty-four-hour operations.
2. Communications
   - To determine the ability to establish and maintain communications essential to support response to an incident/accident.
   - To demonstrate the ability to establish, use, maintain, and manage communications essential to support emergency or disaster response and recovery.
3. Coordination and control
   - To determine the effectiveness of mutual aid plans and the coordination among jurisdictions or organizations if responding to a major emergency.
4. Problem identification and resolution
   - To assess how emergency leadership teams identify, prioritize, and progressively resolve problems tracking problem resolution and retaining an inventory of problems addressed.

5. Leadership
   - To examine how leaders assigned work, tracked taskers, resolved problems, and dealt with unexpected issues during the emergency using the full measure of support resources available.

     More specifically, tabletops can work best when they help pinpoint simultaneous activities and decisions which are often overlooked as ongoing and rapidly evolving crises are managed. These items include ...
   - To determine the effectiveness of procedures for requesting resources from a higher level of government.
   - To determine the level of cooperation and coordination between agencies, departments, and organizations of the jurisdiction in responding to problems associated with a major emergency or disaster.
   - To determine the ability of EOC personnel to assess events, make decisions on corrective action measures, and direct field personnel on procedures to remedy problems.
   - To determine the level of knowledge that EOC personnel possess regarding plan familiarity, emergency operations, and decision making.
   - To determine the capabilities of the jurisdiction to effectively utilize support agencies when local forces are fully committed or incapable of providing a needed service.
   - To determine the adequacy of facilities, equipment, displays, and other materials to support emergency operations.
   - To determine the ability to direct, coordinate, and control emergency response activities through operations of an incident command system (ICS).
   - To demonstrate the capability to direct, coordinate, and control emergency response and recovery operations.
   - To demonstrate the adequacy of facilities, equipment, displays, and associated materials to support direction and control of emergency operations.
6. Emergency public information
   - To determine the capability of the emergency public information system to provide official information and instruction to diverse populations in order to facilitate timely and appropriate public response during a major emergency or disaster.
   - To demonstrate the capability to coordinate the formulation and dissemination of clear, accurate, and consistent information to the public and news media, and to control the spread of rumors that could impact on the public safety.
7. Damage assessment
   - To demonstrate the ability to organize and conduct damage assessment after a major emergency or disaster, and implement follow-up procedures to facilitate response and recovery.

8. Health and medical
   - To determine the ability to protect emergency responder health and safety.
     Most importantly, to oversee and coordinate the staging and support required by public health institutions to meet the emergency needs of citizens and victims in relation to identified emergency cicumstances. Also to assess how essential components of the emergency public health system actually operate under crisis conditions.
   - To determine the ability to implement appropriate measures for containment, recovery, and cleanup of a release of a hazardous material.
   - To determine the adequacy of personnel, procedures, equipment, and vehicles for transporting injured individuals, and the adequacy of medical personnel and facilities to support the operation.
   - To demonstrate the capability to mobilize and employ health and medical resources and mitigate public health problems during a major emergency or mass disaster situation.
   - To demonstrate the capability to take actions required for initial assessment and response to an identified radiological emergency.
   - To demonstrate the capability to identify and mobilize resources and organize the delivery of crisis assistance and other human services in response to a major emergency or disaster.
9. Individual/family assessment
   - To determine the adequacy of the evacuation plan for the jurisdiction and the ability of officials to effectively coordinate an evacuation.
   - To determine the adequacy of procedures for establishing and operating emergency shelters for evacuees.
   - To determine the adequacy of procedures for ensuring the safety and health of persons at emergency shelters.
   - To demonstrate the capability to make decisions for population protection and the adequacy of procedures and capabilities to implement those decisions under emergency or disaster conditions.
   - To demonstrate the capability and procedures to provide facilities and operating resources for the reception, registration, and congregate care of persons displaced from their homes or lodgings by an emergency or disaster.
10. Public safety
    - To determine the effectiveness of search and rescue procedures during a major emergency or disaster.
    - To determine the capabilities of the fire/rescue department to effectively perform fire fighting, rescue, hazardous materials containment, and similar hazard abatement duties during a major emergency or disaster.
    - To determine the adequacy of procedures for limiting access to hazardous/evacuated areas and key governmental facilities and to provide security for the same.

- To determine the adequacy of the reentry decision process following an evacuation.
- To determine the organizational ability and resources necessary to implement site security and to control traffic flow.
- To determine the ability to identify the hazardous material(s) involved in an incident/accident and to access the hazards associated with the material involved during both the emergency and post-emergency phases.
- To demonstrate the capabilities of fire/rescue agencies to effectively respond to firefighting, rescue, and hazardous materials threats which occur during a major emergency or disaster.
- To demonstrate the capability to organize and direct urban search and rescue activities, develop priorities for urban search and rescue support, and manage the mission assignment of federal urban search and rescue forces in response to a catastrophic disaster.
- To demonstrate the capability to maintain law and order, provide evacuation traffic direction and flow control, and provide security and access control at shelters, vital facilities, and evacuated areas.

11. Public works
    - To determine the adequacy of procedures for providing to field forces such support services as food and refreshments, apparatus and equipment maintenance, sanitary facilities, and medical care.
    - To determine the adequacy of procedures for restoring and repairing essential services and vital facilities during a major emergency or disaster.
    - To demonstrate the capability to organize and provide emergency repair and restoration of public works, public utilities, and other critical facilities; debris clearance; and other emergency protective measures in response to a major emergency or disaster.

12. Resource management
    - To determine the thoroughness, usefulness, understandability, and accuracy of the emergency operations plan and other key references.
    - To determine the effectiveness of procedures for deployment of emergency personnel and equipment during a major emergency or disaster.
    - To determine adequacy of procedures for replacement of fatigued personnel during an emergency or disaster.
    - To determine if a system has been developed for recruiting, training, and using volunteers during a major emergency or disaster.
    - To determine the capabilities of agencies, departments, and organizations of the jurisdiction to effectively handle emergencies involving any natural, technological, or man-made hazard.
    - To determine the ability of public officials to conduct their duties in accordance with standard operating procedures (SOPs), the emergency operations plan (EOP), and state statutes.

- To demonstrate the ability to locate, mobilize, and manage (including allocation and prioritization) personnel, equipment, supplies, facilities, and services under emergency or disaster conditions.
13. Warning
    - To demonstrate the capability to promptly alert and notify the public of imminent disaster or hazardous conditions and to disseminate instructional messages to the public on the basis of authority from, or decisions by, appropriate state and local officials.
14. Effectiveness of warning
    - To determine the adequacy of equipment and procedures for alerting and warning the population in the event of a major emergency or disaster.
15. Other nonemergency objectives
    - To determine if officials have coordinated utility disaster plans with the local EOP or with relevant state and county agencies.
    - To determine the capabilities of the jurisdiction to handle routine/normal incidents in addition to responding to events associated with a major emergency event.

The above is a partial listing of functional areas to be tested in a tabletop exercise. It is crucial that cities and states determine how ready they are to handle a range of expected and unexpected scenarios involving natural disasters, hazmat events, and terrorism. Scenarios that challenge the capabilities and readiness of units and their personnel along with their key leaders provide useful insights for achieving higher levels of readiness and overall professional performance.

SAMPLE SCENARIOS

1. Tornado—Dodge City
2. Flash Flood—Public Information
3. Airplane Crash
4. Hazmat Accident—Truck Crash

Tornado-Dodge City

The town of Dodge City is composed of 40,000 people and is located in the upper Red River basin. Due to the fertile soil in the region, farming is one of the main sources of income. There is one local co-op in the city and it is located in the industrial park, approximately one block from the Rapid River. The co-op received a semi load of fertilizers and seeds yesterday to meet the demands of the upcoming growing season.

The Rapid River flows from north to south and has experienced slow-rise flooding in the recent past due to heavy rains. The river is currently within its banks. At the south end of the city, is an independent living complex, which includes, two buildings of assisted-living units. Located to the east of the river is a skilled nursing facility with one hundred residents. Located to the west of the river are two elementary schools and the city water treatment plant.

At 1:45 PM on Wednesday, April 30, the National Weather Service issued a tornado warning for the city. At 1:55 PM a tornado strikes the city, uprooting trees, breaking limbs, and damaging private and public property. Traffic has come to a halt due to downed power lines, trees, and traffic signals. Most telephone lines are also out. Initial damage reports reveal approximately one-half of the city streets are blocked. Some residents are trapped in cars and residences. There is an unconfirmed report that the skilled nursing home sustained damage.

You are receiving reports of a significant amount of dead fish floating in the river. You also receive a report that the co-op roof has been blown off and numerous fertilizer bags have been found in and near the river. Large propane tanks located at the o-op were also impacted, however the extent of the damage is unknown.

There is a 70 percent chance of rain for the next twenty-four-hour period. Temperatures: High 65°F, low 42°F. Winds: Possible gusts up to 40 mph, average 10–20 mph for the next seventy-two hours

Questions

1. As emergency manager what are the most important first steps?
2. What resources should be called upon first?
3. Should you be alerting neighboring towns and state officials?
4. What can be done to mitigate further storm damage?

Flash Flood—Public Information

You have just learned that the National Weather Service has issued a flash-flood warning for the portion of the Yakima River that runs through your county. The vulnerable area is primarily residential but also includes a recreational picnic area alongside the river and one public school. You are also aware of small industrial operations in the valley south of town that may be vulnerable but you have no information on the number of persons who may be in harm's way.

At this time, there is no flooding. However, the school day is almost over and you decide to evacuate the one-floor school, which has about 133 students inside. You must also disseminate the flood warning messages to the community.

Issues

1. What technologies could you use to distribute the evacuation order and warning?
2. Within this specific situation, you have a variety of messages to communicate to different audiences. Draft your message and identify what method you would use to send each message:
   • School occupants must evacuate.
   • Area residents should heed the warning and evacuate.
   • Motorists should avoid the area.
   • Park patrons should evacuate.
   • Parents must be informed that their children have been evacuated.

Airplane Crash

A Boeing-727 aircraft takes off from Kansas City's airport during a raging thunderstorm. As it is climbing, it encounters turbulence, several lightning strikes and a wind shear condition at an altitude of 250 feet. Within seconds, the plane slams into a commercial/residential area three-quarters of a mile south of the airport. Upon impact, the plane is torn apart and leaking jet fuel ignites. Dozens of stores, warehouses, and single-family homes are destroyed over a three-block area. There are numerous injuries and fatalities among passengers and people on the ground.

Fire/rescue units from the city and the airport respond to the scene. They encounter a situation that will require their full resources and capabilities. Additional fire/rescue and police units are requested, as well as the fire mobile command post. Onlookers and media personnel have arrived and are standing too close to the hazardous area as well as interfering with incident response operations.

Questions

1. Where are additional response resources available?
2. How will the services of many agencies and jurisdictions responding be coordinated?
3. How will you deal with the crowds and the media?
4. How will you warn the public to stay away from the crash site?
5. How will you obtain the heavy equipment to assist with the clearing of roadway debris and rescue operations?

6. How will the victims be treated and transported to hospitals?
7. Where will the deceased be taken?
8. Who and what agencies will disseminate official information to the public?
9. What arrangements and agencies will be involved for dealing with relatives of the victims?

HAZMAT MATERIAL ACCIDENT—TRUCK CRASH WITH POTASSIUM PHOSPHIDE LEAK

Thursday, April 23, 2:00 PM

It is a pleasant afternoon in the village of Butler. The temperature is in the upper sixties under partly cloudy skies; a very slight breeze is wafting out of the north at one to two knots. A tanker carrying potassium phosphide is traveling southbound on Twelfth Street. As the truck approaches the intersection at Custer Street, a passenger van rolls through the stop sign on to Twelfth Street into the tanker's path. To avoid a collision, the tanker makes a hard left, careening off the van, losing control, and rolls over onto its side on the northwest side of the intersection. The van is tossed to its side and spins to a stop in the middle of Twelfth Street.

2:08 PM

As the Butler fire trucks roll to a stop at the scene of the crash, they note that the tanker is on its side, and is near the riverbank. A live wire dangling from the power pole is dancing near the wreckage. A visual assessment of the van reveals six occupants. There is little movement in the van or the truck, which contains only the driver. As crews tend to the injured the firefighters begin offloading the hoses to douse the tipped tanker near its gas tank area and prevent an explosion.

2:12 PM

The casualties have been removed from both vehicles. The van's driver is declared dead at the scene; the five passengers (three adults and two children ages eight and ten years old) are found to be developmentally disabled. Two of the adults are unconscious; the other adult, who is secured to a wheelchair, is delirious and having extreme difficulty communicating. All of them are in need of immediate hospitalization, as is the tanker driver. Firefighters have yet to determine what the tanker was carrying and have suspended splashing the tanker completely until they can determine its cargo.

2:29 PM

Word of the accident has spread throughout the village. Calls are coming into the police and fire departments. Visitors numbering several dozens and the media are crowding the village hall and the perimeter of the crash scene; both groups are growing increasingly concerned and demanding the hazardous material be cleaned up quickly and some determination be made about whether the accident scene is safe again for normal activity.

Questions

1. Is the fire response correct?
2. What additional precautions are needed?
3. Should the accident area be immediately cleared of onlookers?

EXERCISE EVALUATION (SAMPLE)

Tabletop Participant Feedback

Exercise Name:_____ Date: _____

Location of Exercise_____ County: _____

Participant Role: Player Observer Facilitator

Participant Name: _____ Title: _____

Agency: _____

	Ineffective	Satisfactory	Highly Effective
Exercise organization			
1. Exercise objectives	[ ]	[ ]	[ ]
2. Exercise MSEL	[ ]	[ ]	[ ]
3. Response cell actions	[ ]	[ ]	[ ]
4. Exercise environment/ facilities	[ ]	[ ]	[ ]
5. Exercise communications	[ ]	[ ]	[ ]
Exercise Play			
1. Player performance	[ ]	[ ]	[ ]
2. Completion of assigned taskers	[ ]	[ ]	[ ]
3. Resolution of novel problems	[ ]	[ ]	[ ]
4. Response to incoming messages	[ ]	[ ]	[ ]

5. Leadership   [ ]   [ ]   [ ]
6. Team coordination   [ ]   [ ]   [ ]
7. Team collaboration with   [ ]   [ ]   [ ]
     others
8. Interagency communications [ ]   [ ]   [ ]
9. Use of relevant technologies [ ]   [ ]   [ ]

Recommendations and Action steps

1. Based on discussions today and the issues identified, list the top three issues and/or areas that need improvement.

     _____

     _____

     _____

     _____

     _____

2. Identify corrective steps that should be taken to address the issues identified above. For each corrective step, indicate if it is a high, medium, or low priority.

     _____

     _____

     _____

     _____

     _____

3. Describe the corrective steps that should be taken in your agency. Who should be assigned responsibility for each action item?

     _____

     _____

     _____

     _____

     _____

4. List the policies, plans, and procedures that should be reviewed, revised, or developed. Indicate the priority level for each.

     _____

     _____

     _____

     _____

     _____

5. What parts of the exercise went very well and proved very effective?
   Which parts did not?
   1. _____
   2. _____
   3. _____

6. Explain what portions or elements of the EOP need revision based on
   exercise results?

   _____
   _____
   _____
   _____
   _____

Appendix E

Useful Resources

HSEEP—The Homeland Security Exercise and Evaluation Program emphasizes and embraces a "building block approach" in emergency exercise program management and supports the value of progression by exposing program participants to gradually increasing exercise complexity. The HSEEP asserts that increasing complexity leads to increasing capabilities. An additional HSEEP function is to standardize the language and concepts used by various agencies and organizations in the emergency exercise planning process. (Gebbie & Valas, 2006).

Green's text—Green's *Exercise Alternatives for Training Emergency Management Command Center Staffs* advocates emergency exercise progression through a structured series of learning events, from the known to the unknown and from the simple to the complex. This is a foundation and principle of adult learning that will enable emergency management participants to learn the most effectively. Increasingly complex exercises lead to greater involvement and advancing emergency management functional skills. Additionally, Green asserts, "gradual progression" also allows for increased flexibility, such as greater ability to vary exercise characteristics based on the participants' experience levels; a greater range of exercise training program participant involvement options (e.g., individual/ self-directed learning, individual/classroom training, team training, and systems training); increased training venue (i.e., office, home, and the Internet) options; and training schedules (to include "just-in-time training," which is training just prior to a major event and training as frequently as once a week).

DHS HSPDs—The national framework for emergency preparedness began with Homeland Security Presidential Directive 5 (HSPD-5, February 2003), which directed the development of the National Response Plan (NRP). This plan aligned federal coordination, capabilities, and resources into a multidiscipline, all-hazards approach under a comprehensive incident management system known as the National Incident Management System (NIMS). HSPD-5 was followed by Homeland Security Presidential Directive 8 (HSPD-8, December 2003), which put forth the following National Preparedness Goal: "establishing mechanisms for improved delivery of Federal preparedness assistance to State and local governments" (www. LLIS.gov). Further, the National Preparedness Goal prescribes a capabilities-based planning approach for a wide range of threats and hazards. The Universal Task List (UTL) is a tool to assist the homeland security community to implement the capabilities-based planning process established under HSPD-8. It is a "living" document that is continually evolving and expanding as it is put into practice.

Issuance of all HSPD documents since 2002 should be reviewed and cataloged to deal with the range of issues raised in this book. Looking at the NIMS, the NIPP and the variety of ESF functions is also crucial. In this way the rudimentary features of emergency preparedness and response standards can be articulated and clarified. Take advantage of research, new items, books and periodicals which depict breakthroughs and refinements in overall emergency planning, preparedness and response. This is an area where shared insights and learning contributes to the quality of emergency management in every city and town.

NFPA standards—This codification of performance and safety standards has been developed by the National Fire Protection Association for the measurement of actual task activities by first responders where metrics and measures of calibrated effort are spelled out for reference to enable judgments about player performance during an exercise.

DISCUSSION-BASED EXERCISES

Seminar

The seminar is an informal discussion that is used to orient participants to plans, policies, or procedures that are new or updated. An LPHA may conduct a seminar under a variety of circumstances, including the initiation of a new plan, procedure, or mutual aid agreement, or in the event of new staffing, leadership, facilities, or risk(s). No previous experience is needed, and minimal staff preparation and lead time are required. Seminars make use of various training techniques including lectures, films, slides, and videotapes.

Workshop

The workshop is similar to a seminar but is done to produce certain products, for example, to draft plan or policy. Workshops are often conducted when developing a large scale exercise or a multiyear exercise plan. Similar to seminars, it makes use of various training techniques that include lectures, films, slides, videotapes, and panel discussions.

Tabletop Exercise (TTX)

A TTX is a low-stress event to stimulate discussion of a simulated situation. Participants discuss issues in depth. TTXs are designed as an early step along the way to functional and full-scale exercises. Constructive problem solving is the goal of such an exercise. A copy of the appropriate emergency plan and other pertinent materials are available for reference during a TTX. A staff person is assigned to act as recorder, documenting actions taken during a TTX; these notations serve as a reference tool for evaluating the exercise.

A TTX typically begins with a briefing by the facilitator to orient participants and simulators to the TTX objectives, ground rules, and communication and simulation procedures. The scenario narrative is then presented in an intelligence briefing. The scenario is generally invented and describes an event or emergency incident, bringing participants up to a simulated "present moment" in time. The selected event should be one that is realistic for the first responders (e.g., a hurricane on the eastern seaboard, a transportation event at a major railroad hub). Materials may be distributed to provide details about an imaginary jurisdiction, or participants may be instructed to use their knowledge of actual local resources. The facilitator announces the beginning and end of the exercise and introduces the first problem, along with subsequent pacing messages, to the participants.

Games

The game is a simulation of operations that uses rules, data, and procedures designed to depict an actual or potential real-life situation. It often involves two or more teams simulating a competitive environment and is slightly more complex than the tabletop exercise. The goal of a game is to explore decision-making processes. As the game proceeds decisions are made and in turn the sequence of events affects those decisions. Participants of a game also explore the consequences of their decisions.

OPERATIONS-BASED EXERCISES

Drill

The purpose of a drill is to use repetition to instruct thoroughly. Drills can be used to test personnel training, response time, interagency cooperation and resources, and workforce and equipment capabilities. Drills optimally take place after orientation; staff should have an understanding of the agency function that will be tested in the drill and be given an opportunity to ask questions. How a drill begins depends on the type of drill being conducted. Drill categories include but are not limited to notification, communication, command post, and evacuation. In most cases, a general briefing by the drill designer sets the scene and reviews the drill's purpose and objectives. Operational procedures and safety precautions are reviewed before the drill begins. Personnel are required to report, either in person or by telephone or e-mail, to a designated drill site or contact location. Both planned and spontaneous messages sustain the drill's action.

Functional Exercise (FE)

The purpose of an FE is to test and evaluate the capabilities of an emergency response system. Events and situations that would actually occur over an extended period of time are depicted or described. Time transitions advance the activity while staying within the time allotted for the exercise (e.g., "It is now twenty-four hours later"). The objectives of an FE determine how it is to be organized. For example, a "no-notice" exercise does not have a start time; in such an exercise, the objectives would include testing staff members' ability to move into their emergency response roles and activities quickly and efficiently. Other FEs, however, may be announced in advance. Immediately before the start of the FE, participants are briefed on the objectives, procedures, time frame, and recording requirements. FEs depend on reaction to simulated information delivered by paper, telephone, or radio to individuals or agencies that must then coordinate responses with other players. These messages can be prescripted or developed by the simulation cell during the course of the exercise.

Full-Scale Deployed Exercise (FSDE)

The purpose of an FSDE is to test and evaluate a major portion of the emergency operations plan in an interactive manner over an extended period. FSDEs typically involve more than one agency for several days. As with an FE, the objectives of an FSDE must be specified, and the actual exercise begins with a simulated event that prompts the initiation of the plan. An FSDE differs from a functional drill in that field personnel from the participating agencies physically proceed to the location of the mock emergency. The FSDE includes all of the activities taking place at the emergency operations center (EOC) as well as on-scene use of simulated victims, equipment, and workforce. Activities at the scene serve as input and require coordination with the EOC. An FSDE combines the planned and spontaneous messages characteristic of FEs with actions from the field. Together, the FSDE is the most complex, costly, and realistic of all the exercise options and carries significant risks for safety and security, which must be constantly managed.

ORGANIZATION OF THE EXERCISE PLANNING TEAM

The Exercise Planning Team's responsibilities include design, structure, coordination, and overall management of the exercise. Team size will depend on the size of the organization or agency to be exercised and should be modified to fit the scope and scale of ordinary operations. The roles and responsibilities for the planning team must be clearly defined and should include delegation of responsibilities among team members as described below.

Exercise director/controller—Assigns tasks and responsibilities, establishes the timeline, and guides and monitors exercise development. Typically, this role consists of a single team leader whose technical expertise puts him/her in charge of overall operations. The director will usually serve as controller to ensure a stable and steady direction for the exercise from STARTEX to ENDEX.

Operations—Ensures scenario accuracy and applicability, and develops the evaluation criteria. Participants in this group typically include departmental subject matter experts, and requisite technical experts are available or on call for response cell work or MSEL tasker development.

Planning—Collects and reviews all policies and procedures applicable to the exercise. Also develops simulation and *injects* (i.e., intermediate changes or challenges to the exercise participants) needed to sustain exercise flow. In small departments or for small-scale exercises, the planning group may be combined with the operations group. Planners work with others on the following tasks:

1. Setting a timeline for the planning process
2. Defining the exercise's purpose
3. Selecting the scenario, goals, and objectives for the exercise
4. Scheduling events, location, date, time, and duration of the exercise

5. Defining exercise control and preparing all documentation and exercise materials
6. Facilitating exercise organization, including communication needs, rules of conduct, security and safety issues
7. Arranging logistics (e.g., parking, assembly areas, transportation, restrooms, food/water for participants, maps and directions, etc.)
8. Providing training on responsibilities/activities of the team, exercise participants, and evaluators

Administration/finance—Keeps an account of the costs involved in conducting an exercise. For small agencies, this group may consist of a single individual, who may be the same administrative support person assigned to the logistics role.

Appendix F

Information Sharing and Message Management

Coordinating and tracking the exchange, receipt, transmission, interpretation and execution of emergency communications is not an open and shut case. Planning prior to crises is essential to map out how critical information flows ought to be processed and executed. This entails direct communication between the Incident Commander, the EOC, the state or federal officials who may be augmenting response and other emergency responders brought in under an EMAD (Emergency Management Assistance Compact).

Issues involve the specific technology to be used, frequencies, call signs, signals, special codes as well as careful analysis of the message itself. For example, did the message under review

- ask for information?
- provide information?
- ask for clarification?
- ask for assistance?
- inquire about an update?
- provide an update?
- assign a tasking?
- respond to a tasking?

Are there strict time limits? Are there special technical issues or requirements? Does the message require multiple recipients? Can the message to be widely shared? Narrowly shared? Why? Should the message be simply stored for reference?

Information flow analysis, especially of information sharing requirements among key players must be considered because of the valuable insights it generates about who really needs information, how that information gets to those who need it, the barriers involved and the measures one can take to enhance information sharing in a real crisis. This should be done by staging a low-key tabletop exercise to involve all key players and examine the information needs during the first 4 hours of a crisis using differential scenarios to sort out what information issues seem most important.

MESSAGE MANGEMENT

Once information sharing is better understood through the tabletop exercise, more intensive reviews of how messages are managed during the course of complex crises can be captured and understood. Which messages get priority? Why? Which ones tend to be neglected—why?

What is the role of the EOC in message management? How should written logs and electronic logs be used? Which messages tend to misinterpreted— why? What measures can be instituted to maximize effective message flow, enable tracking responses, determine how and when execution tasks have been completed? What can we learn from other jurisdictions, organizations and experts about improving the overall management of messages in a crisis?

The overall relationship between information sharing and message management cannot be understated although it is often overlooked. Real investments of time and attentive energy can provide dividends for those emergency managers willing to take a closer look at these issues.

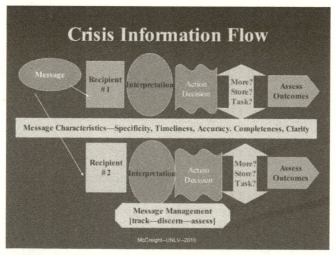

Figure F.1   The Flow of Information and Messaging in a Crisis.

Bibliography

Alexander, D. (2003). Towards the development of standards in emergency management training and education. *Disaster Prevention and Management, 12,* 113–23.

Federal Emergency Management Agency (2003). *IS-139 exercise design.*

Federal Emergency Management Agency, Emergency Management Institute. http://train- ing.fema.gov/EMIWeb/IS/is139lst.asp (Retrieved January 17, 2009).

Gebbie, K., and Valas, J. (2006). *Planning, designing, conducting, and evaluating local public health emergency exercises.* New York: Columbia University Press.

Green, W., III. (2000). *Exercise alternatives for training emergency management command center staffs.* Boca Raton, FL: Universal.

Homeland Security Exercise and Evaluation Program. (n.d.). *Mission and exercise types.* https://hseep.dhs.gov (retrieved January 17, 2009).

Lurie, N., Nelson, C., and Wasserman, J. (2007). Assessing public health emergency preparedness: Concepts, tools, and challenges. *Annual Review of Public Health, 28,* 1–18.

Perry, R., and Lindell, M. (2003). Preparedness for emergency response: Guidelines for the emergency planning process. *Disasters, 27,* 336–50.

Quarantelli, E. (1997). Ten criteria for evaluating the management of community disasters. *Disasters, 21,* 39–56.

U.S. Department of Homeland Security. (n.d.). *HSEEP training course: Participants manual.* Washington, DC: Author.

Index

About the Author

After serving the United States government at the State Department and other federal agencies over a 35 year career, Dr. McCreight retired in 2004 and served as a consultant for major homeland security and national defense contractors. His professional career includes work as an intelligence analyst, treaty negotiator, arms control delegate to the UN, counter-terrorism advisor, political-military affairs analyst and Deputy Director of Global Scientific Exchanges at State Department. During his service at State Department he was a senior Soviet military analyst with INR and specialized in the assessment of nuclear, chemical and biological weapons programs. Later in his professional career he performed assignments where he either managed or coordinated international post-disaster relief and humanitarian operations, developed peacekeeping policy, promoted global science and technology cooperation projects, and helped design treaty verification systems.

At the middle of his career he also participated in the design and coordination of White House nuclear readiness command crisis exercises during the Reagan administration. During his federal career he designed, developed and coordinated well over twenty-six cabinet level strategic nuclear preparedness exercises, worked on Presidential Protection and Survivability Programs and directed the operation of several dozen senior-level military exercises involving theoretical force-on-force scenarios between the United States and the Soviet Union. This followed several years of designing and evaluating unit combat exercises for the U.S. Army.

McCreight spent twenty-seven years of combined active and reserve military service concurrently with his civilian work in U.S. Army Special Operations and has devoted fifteen years to teaching graduate school as an adjunct at Georgetown, George Mason, George Washington, and Virginia Tech Universities in subjects as diverse as disaster and emergency management, strategic intelligence, nonproliferation policy, homeland security policies, terrorism analysis, intelligence analysis, scientific issues and defense policy and assessing WMD threats. He completed his doctoral degree in Public Administration in 1989 and remains active in graduate education programs in emergency and crisis management as well as security studies and terrorism analysis. He has also written and published over thirty-five articles on chemical weapons use, disaster management, disaster recovery, post-strike attribution, biological weapons threats to homeland security, crisis management, WMD scenario development and collegiate educational strategies for developing future crisis managers for government service. His second edition of this textbook—*Emergency Exercise Design and Evaluation* was published in 2016 and became a popular resource in both undergraduate and graduate schools. He has co-edited and authored a new textbook on Homeland Defense published by CRC Press in October 2014.

CPSIA information can be obtained
at www.ICGtesting.com
Printed in the USA
LVHW112303281119
638903LV00006B/20/P